GOD WROTE A BOOK

GOD
WROTE A BOOK

JAMES MACDONALD

CROSSWAY

WHEATON, ILLINOIS

Trade paperback ISBN: 978-1-58134-622-0

Mobipocket ISBN: 978-1-4335-1083-0

PDF ISBN: 978-1-4335-1082-3

Library of Congress Cataloging-in-Publication Data
MacDonald, James, 1960-
    God wrote a book / James MacDonald.
      p. cm.
    Includes bibliographical references.
    ISBN 13: 978-1-58134-622-0
    ISBN 10: 1-58134-622-0
    1.Bible—Evidences, authority, etc. I. Title.
BS480 .M27   2002
220.1—dc21   2002008184

Crossway is a publishing ministry of Good News Publishers.

VP		19	18	17	16	15	14	13
18	17	16	15	14	13	12	11	10	9

*To Judy Van Kampen, Scott Pierre, and
Karla Van Kampen Pierre,
who have given of themselves generously and tirelessly
to promote and proclaim the book God wrote.
Sola Scriptura*

CONTENTS

INTRODUCTION

The grass withers, the flower fades, but the
word of our God stands forever.

ISAIAH 40:8

Wow, so you're really going to do it? You're going to read a book about the Bible and why you should seriously consider what it says. What would your friends say? Why are you doing this? Is it because you have a passionate curiosity about an amazing number of things, and it's just time to take a look at the Bible? Maybe you have been feeling an emptiness in your life, something missing, and you respect someone who believes the Bible. Or could it be that a family member has given you this book because that person wants you to have a faith like his or hers? Are you feeling pressure to read this book and doing it out of obligation, or is it something you are choosing to do for yourself?

Well, guess what? It really doesn't matter to me. I'm just glad you are where you are, because I believe this could be a major turning point in your life. Something you will look back on for many years as the day when something incredibly exciting and fulfilling began for you.

I simply want to share with you what the Bible is and what it can do for you. I'm not asking you to get all emotional and weird. I'm not asking you to check your intellect at the door. Quite the contrary — I'm asking you to engage your mind and consider the evidence for the Bible as a supernatural book.

As for me, I'm not sharing from the perspective of a theoretician, and I'm not claiming to be objective. I'm a satisfied customer, and the material I have written is very convincing to me. But I will try to avoid the kind of high-pressure, "hard-sell" stuff that we all hate, especially in matters of religion. Instead, I have written in a very personal tone. The English is not formal. It's just the way we would talk if we were sitting on a bench in a park somewhere.

If what I have written is accurate, then there are implications for you, but I will leave that to the end and mostly to you personally. So let me just begin by saying this: God did write a book, and it's definitely not this one. However, if you understand and agree with the message of this book, it can be a bridge for you to the greatest book ever written. And that alone makes it worth the two to three hours it will take to read it. Okay?

Let's get at it!

1

Evidence for the Bible You Shouldn't Ignore

But [Jesus] answered and said, "It is written,
'Man shall not live on bread alone, but on every
word that proceeds out of the mouth of God.'"

MATTHEW 4:4

To most people in our world today the Bible is an ancient book with little practical relevance for life in the twenty-first century. If they have a Bible, it just sits and collects dust with a lot of other books they own and have never seriously read. Like a secret treasure buried in their own backyard, the majority allow this book to sit silently at the back of their consciousness. These people never dream how near they are to incredible wealth. Having talked to people all over the world about this subject, I can tell you that their reasons for ignoring the

Bible are surprisingly similar and disturbingly weak. In fact, we recently surveyed 100 people with this request: Name a common reason people give for ignoring the Bible. Here are the top five:

- "The Bible is just a bunch of stories. Noah's ark? Adam and Eve? Yeah, right! And Superman and Cinderella too, I suppose?"
- "The Bible is filled with contradictions. How can I take a book seriously that doesn't even agree with itself? One guy says this; another guy says that; get your act together, boys!"
- "The Bible is outdated. I don't respect people from 200 years ago; so what could I possibly learn from a book that was written more than 2,000 years ago?"
- "I believe that an individual's faith is a very personal matter; it's different for each person. You don't get that from a book. It comes from deep within."
- "The Bible is not scientific. It's filled with all kinds of inaccuracies that are offensive to the modern intellectual. Only the most naive and simplistic could ever take seriously a book written by a bunch of fishermen or whatever."

Pretty good survey, right? As you can tell, I have been talking to a lot of people about the Bible. Did you see your primary objection on the list? Well . . . now hear this: NONE of those things is true, and if you keep reading, I believe I can prove it to you. Contrary to popular opinion, there is incredible evidence for the uniqueness and reliability of the Bible. Yes, evidence!

EXTERNAL EVIDENCE

By external evidence, we mean proofs that exist outside the Bible. Some people might say, "Using the Bible to prove the Bible is circular reasoning." There is some truth to that. That's why we are going to examine several proofs outside the Bible to show that it's a supernatural book. Then we will get into what the Bible says about itself.

Preeminence Among Literature

First, the Bible is paramount in the world of literature. Even if you don't accept it as God's book, it is absolutely irrefutable that the Bible stands alone among all other books—by far! Ecclesiastes says that **"the writing of many books is endless" (Ecclesiastes 12:12)**, but stack up all the books ever written—ancient and modern—and the Bible is unsurpassed. In fact, don't even put the Bible on top. It is so far above and beyond any book ever written that it needs to go in a separate pile. It is preeminent. Let me give you some specifics.

1. *The Bible is preeminent in its circulation.* The Bible has been read by more people in more languages than any other book in human history. The entire Bible is now translated into more than 400 languages, and portions of it have been translated into nearly 2,500 languages.[1] Many of these languages would not even have a written form if Bible translators had not first learned the language, developed a grammar and dictionary for that language, and then translated the Bible into it.

Here are some numbers that blew my mind. The United Bible Societies report that their network of organizations distributed 633 million portions of Scripture throughout the world in the year 2000.[2] In 2001 The Gideons International placed and distributed more than 56 million complete copies of God's Word worldwide.[3] That averages more than one million copies every week—107 copies a minute! With a total circulation well into the tens of billions, the Bible is definitely preeminent in its circulation.

2. *The Bible is preeminent in its influence.* The Bible's influence on other books is incalculable. More books have been written about the Bible than any other subject,

and more authors quote the Bible than any other source. Christian apologist Bernard Ramm said:

> From the Apostolic Fathers dating from A.D. 95 to modern times, there is one great literary river inspired by the Bible — Bible dictionaries, Bible encyclopedias, Bible lexicons, Bible atlases, and Bible geographies. These may be taken as a starter. Then at random we may mention the vast bibliographies around theology, religious education, hymnology, missions, the biblical languages, church history, religious biography, devotional works, commentaries, philosophy of religion, evidences, apologetics, and on and on. There seems to be an endless number.[4]

3. *The Bible is preeminent among religious writings.* You say, "Hang on for a minute. The Bible may be a great religious book, but what about the Qur'an? What about the Book of Mormon? What about books on Eastern religions?" Professor M. Montiero Williams (not to be confused with Montel Williams) was the Boden Professor of Sanskrit at Oxford University during the latter half of the nineteenth century. He spent forty-two years studying Eastern religious books. Comparing them to the Bible, he said:

> Pile them, if you will, on the left side of your study table; but place your own Holy Bible on the right side — all by itself, all alone — and with a wide gap

between them. For there is a gulf between it and the so-called sacred books of the East, which severs the one from the other utterly, hopelessly, and forever . . . a veritable gulf which cannot be bridged over by any science or religious thought.[5]

The Bible is preeminent. There is no book on the face of the earth that comes anywhere close. Saying that any book, anywhere, written by anyone, could on any level compare to the Bible would be a statement of ignorance. A knowing person, a studied person, a person who has examined the subject objectively and carefully could never say that; the proof is so overwhelming. The first piece of external evidence for the Bible as God's Word is its preeminence among literature.

Preservation Under Attack

Here is the second piece of evidence: The Bible's preservation from its enemies. It goes without saying that the Bible is ever and always under attack. Since the Old and New Testaments were written, people have given their lives to destroy God's Word. The irrefutable record of the Bible's survival despite this onslaught is evidence that it is a supernatural book.

    1. *The attack of man.* No other book has been so burned and banned and outlawed as the Bible. From Roman

emperors to Communist leaders to college professors, many have taken it upon themselves to attack God's book. Why this book? Why are people always attacking the Bible? Travel to any state school in America and try to find someone attacking the Qur'an. No, instead they talk about that book with respect. Check out a secular college campus and try to find someone attacking the Book of Mormon. Why is no one doing that? Because almighty God has only written one book that convicts people of their sin and the necessity of being reconciled to Him.

Here is just one illustration of how the Bible has been preserved under attack. You may have heard of Voltaire, the French infidel. He predicted that Christianity would be destroyed within 100 years of his lifetime and that the only place you'd find a Bible would be in a museum. Instead, Voltaire has become history, and the circulation of the Bible continues to increase around the world. Ironically, within fifty years of Voltaire's death in 1778, the Geneva Bible Society bought his home and used his own printing press to print Bibles.[6] The Bible has been uniquely preserved through human history because God wrote it, and God is one hundred percent committed to taking care of it. Those who set themselves to destroy the Bible are not going against man. They are going against almighty God, and that is why they always fail. I certainly wouldn't want to spend my life trying to get God's book out of circulation. Would you?

2. *The attack of time.* People say, "The Bible is too old. How can we know for sure that we have what was originally written? Hasn't it been corrupted through time?" That's a really good question, and a lot of people are not sure of the answer. Let me walk you through some material that might be new to you, but that is really important.

The word *manuscript* is used to describe the ancient documents upon which Scripture was written and first copied. There are now more than 5,600 ancient manuscripts of the Greek New Testament. Add to that nearly 10,000 Latin manuscripts and 9,300 other early versions, and we have nearly 25,000 early manuscripts of the Bible. No other ancient document even comes close. The next most commonly copied document is Homer's *Iliad* with 643 manuscripts, all of them partial.[7] Thus the Bible manuscripts outnumber those for Homer by nearly forty to one. Now if you were to drive down to your local university and say to an English professor who studies ancient literature, "I don't believe we have a reliable version of Homer's *Iliad*," he would say, "What are you talking about? Of course we do." If 643 manuscripts are sufficient to establish an ancient text, what about 25,000?

How could anyone seriously doubt that we have the original text of the Bible?

Why is that a big deal? Early on, before there was a printing press, very few people had their own Bibles. This book was written on parchment, and it had to be copied and recopied by hand. You couldn't go down to the store and buy one—it was too expensive. You might wonder, "Well, if it was copied so many times, how could it keep from getting messed up?"

That brings us to the second point—the number of variants. As people copied, what if they didn't copy it accurately? How do we know that we have an exact transmission of the Bible as it originally existed? The scribes who copied the Bible took great care in transmitting the text. They counted the words and even the letters to make sure that nothing was omitted. They even had proofreaders who checked their copy against the master copy.

Despite their care, however, inadvertent mistakes sometimes crept into an individual text—differences in punctuation or spelling or misplaced words. Most of these variants are easily accounted for. In fact, less than 1 percent of the words in the New Testament are seriously debated, and none of these affects any doctrine of the faith. As some respected New Testament scholars have declared, ". . . not one fundamental doctrine of the

Christian faith rests on a disputed reading."[8] It is really amazing the way God has preserved His Word. As Sir Frederic G. Kenyon, one of the greatest authorities in the field of New Testament textual criticism, said:

> It cannot be too strongly asserted that in substance the text of the Bible is certain: Especially this is the case with the New Testament. The number of manuscripts of the New Testament, of early translations from it, and of quotations from it in the oldest writers of the Church, is so large that it is practically certain that the true reading of every doubtful passage is preserved in one or another of these ancient authorities. This can be said of no other book in the world.[9]

Thirdly, consider the time gap between the original writing and the earliest copies. I mentioned Homer's *Iliad* above. Although the *Iliad* was written around 800 B.C., the earliest copy we have is from 400 B.C. — a difference of 400 years.[10] Compare that to the New Testament, which was completed no later than A.D. 95.[11] Our earliest New Testament manuscript — a fragment from the Gospel of John — dates from A.D. 125, a span of only thirty years! That's all. The New Testament has an advantage of 370 years in the time between its writing and the first existing copies. And the time gap for Homer's *Iliad* is not nearly as great as some other classic works, such as Herodotus and Plato. The gap for these is often more than 1,000 years.[12] The manuscript evidence for the authority and accuracy of God's Word is incredible. God has preserved His Word. That's why we can invite people to open their Bibles and turn to a certain verse and then share with confidence, "Here's what God says!"

You say, "Well, that's the New Testament. What about the Old Testament?" Good question. The phenomenal thing about the Old Testament is that there is great manuscript evidence for it as well. The Old Testament scribes took great care with the biblical manuscripts. It took hours to copy one page. If they made a single mistake, they had to tear up the whole page and start over. They were meticulous about copying, checking, and then rechecking what they had written.

Critics of the faith used to point out the gap between the original writings of the Old Testament and the earliest existing copies. Since the Old Testament was completed around 400 B.C., and the earliest manuscripts we had were A.D. 900, there was a gap of 1,300 years. That's huge. People would say, for example, "We don't know what the original book of Isaiah said. With such a huge gap, there must have been all kinds of changes." Then in 1947 a large collection of manuscripts came to light near the Dead Sea. This little shepherd kid threw a rock into a cave and heard a crash! He climbed inside to investigate and found documents stored inside earthen jars. The archaeologists found out about this, and over the next several years pulled out 100,000 fragments that were pieced back together into about 800 ancient documents. These came to be known as the Dead Sea Scrolls. It's a marvelous story if you have never read it.

Many of the manuscripts were copies of the Old Testament Scriptures. For example, they found a complete copy of Isaiah that was 1,000 years older than the previous oldest manuscript. People wondered, "What will the real book of Isaiah look like? What will the differences be?" Well, guess what? Scholars examined Isaiah 53, one of the clearest prophecies about Christ, and here is what they found:

> Of the 166 words in Isaiah 53, there are only seventeen letters in question. Ten of these letters are simply a matter of spelling, which does not affect the sense. Four more letters are minor stylistic changes, such as conjunctions. The remaining three letters comprise the word "light," which is added in verse 11, and does not affect the meaning greatly. Furthermore, this word is supported by the LXX [Septuagint]. . . . Thus, in one chapter of 166 words, there is only one word (three letters) in question after a thousand years of

transmission — and this word does not significantly change the meaning of the passage.[13]

Now let me tell you as plainly and simply as I know how that God has preserved His Word. When you pick up the Bible, you are holding in your hands the words of almighty God. Yes, God wrote a book. We would do well to take it very, very seriously.

Proof from Archaeology

The Old Testament especially speaks of hundreds of names and places and events. If you have read the Old Testament, you know that it talks about wars and captivities and geopolitical movements. Opponents of the Bible have said increasingly, "That never happened! There is no such place as this. There is no such place as that." An article in *Christianity Today* a few years ago begged to differ:

> True, no archaeological evidence exists for Abraham, Joseph, or Moses. Revisionist scholars [that is, people who attack the Bible] say this means the Bible stories of Israel's origin are fiction. Yet we have only recently discovered King Solomon's seal, King David's name in stone, and a bull the Canaanites worshipped. Now two leading Egyptologists are marshaling evidence from the land of the Pharaohs to answer the question: Did the Exodus ever happen?[14]

The answer is: "Yes, it did happen." Now go back 100 years to the time when higher criticism was influencing the seminaries in our nation in the 1880s and '90s. Liberals were attacking things in the Bible. An amazing number of discoveries have actually been made that prove how foolish their conclusions were.

Let me give you just a couple of examples of how archaeology has proven the accuracy of Scripture. William Albright, known as one of the greatest archaeologists of his day, said, "There can be no doubt that archaeology has confirmed the substantial historicity of Old Testament tradition." He added:

> The excessive skepticism shown toward the Bible by important historical schools of the eighteenth and nineteenth centuries . . . has been progressively discredited. Discovery after discovery has established the accuracy of innumerable details, and has brought increased recognition to the value of the Bible as a source of history.[15]

Now Albright and some of these other archaeologists are not necessarily Bible-believing Christians. They are just finding support for things that used to be ridiculed by skeptics. They're going over to the Middle East and digging up physical data that confirms the Bible. Then they are like, "Oops. Oh, sorry. Well, um.

Yeah. Okay." It's going on constantly right now in our lifetime—archaeology confirming the message of the Bible.

Let me give you three examples. Critics of the Bible used to say that Moses was not the author of the Pentateuch. "Moses didn't write the first five books of the Bible. People couldn't even write in 1400 B.C. Get real!" They also claimed that the priesthood and the sacrificial system that Moses wrote about developed much later. Then in 1975 the Ebla Tablets were discovered, nearly 20,000 written records dating 1,000 years before the time of Moses. When they were translated, archaeologists found that many of the laws, customs, and sacrificial systems existed long before the time of Moses. Some of the laws and punishments for certain crimes in Scripture actually paralleled the legal thinking of that day.[16] Oops. Maybe Moses did write the Pentateuch.

People used to laugh at Old Testament references to the Hittites, which the Bible mentions approximately fifty times. For years and years you could go to a secular campus around the country, and some professor would stand up in class and say to the young people, "The Hittites. What a joke. There were no Hittites. Archaeologists have been digging over there for years, and those people never existed. They are a fabrication of the Bible."

Oops. Recent archaeological digs have found hundreds of references to the Hittite people. They lived over a 1,200-year period in the Middle East.[17]

Do you remember the story of Laban? When Jacob and Rachel left Laban's home, Rachel stole his family idols or *teraphim* (Genesis 31). Critics of Scripture ridiculed this story for years because it says that when Laban discovered the theft, he pursued the couple over many, many miles. Commentators wondered why he would go to such pains to recover the images he could have easily replaced locally.

Well, in 1925 more than 1,000 clay tablets were found at a site in Mesopotamia called Nuzi. These tablets revealed that a person who possessed the family idols could make a legal claim to all of the family property. In other words, as long as Jacob and Rachel had those statues in their hands, they owned everything that was Laban's.[18] All of a sudden people were saying, "Oh. Now I get it."

There are many things like this about which the Bible doesn't comment or explain; it simply records them because the details were common knowledge among the people to whom those Scriptures were originally written. Now with the discoveries of modern archaeology, those who have ridiculed the historical reliability of the Bible are having to admit that *they* were the ones in error.

Well, that is external evidence: preeminence among literature, preservation under attack, and proof from archaeology. Each of these establishes a strong foundation for confidence in the Bible as a supernatural book. Now let's look at the internal evidence for the Bible as God's Word.

INTERNAL EVIDENCE

Amazing Agreement

One of the things that you have to be struck by when you read the Bible is the amazing agreement among its authors. For instance, do you know how many different people wrote the Bible? It's not one or two people; it's not five or ten people. It's forty people. These forty authors could not be more diverse. Some of them were shepherds. Some of them were political leaders. There were kings. There was a tax collector. There were religious leaders. There were prophets. Notice the variety. Add to that the fact that these people lived over a period of 1,500 years. We can't even get four people who witnessed a traffic accident to agree on the details. How do you get forty different people from different walks of life, separated by 1,500 years, writing about the two things that nobody ever talks about—religion and politics—to agree? I'll tell you how. They were writing down the things that God Himself, the source of all Scripture, led them to write. God did write a book, and the amazing agreement among its human authors is just one of the internal proofs.

Total Consistency

You say, "Well, hang on a cotton-picking minute — everyone knows that the Bible is filled with contradictions." Who told you that? Saying that the Bible is jammed with contradictions is a very serious charge. If the Bible is filled with contradictions, then how could God have written it? What kind of a God could make mistakes? The next time somebody tells you the Bible has a lot of contradictions in it, say, "Name one." Most people won't have anything to say; they are just parroting what someone else has told them. Most who do raise an actual issue with the Bible reveal how very little they have ever studied it. In fact, almost all of the supposed "contradictions" floating around can be resolved by the following:

1. *Supposed contradictions of message.* These are the easiest ones, usually raised by folks who are pretty clueless about the Bible. They will say things such as: "In the Old Testament it says, 'An eye for an eye and a tooth for a tooth.' And in the New Testament it says, 'Turn the other

cheek.' There! What do you think of that?" Then I would say, "Have you ever read the Bible? Jesus totally cleared that up. If you look at the Gospel of Matthew, Jesus said, **"You have heard that it was said, 'An eye for an eye, and a tooth for a tooth.' But I say to you . . . whoever slaps you on your right cheek, turn to him the other also"** (Matthew 5:38-39). There is no message contradiction. It used to be the Old Covenant, written on tablets of stone; now it's the New Covenant, written on the heart (2 Corinthians 3:3).

When my son was ten, he was not allowed to sit in the driver's seat of the car while he waited for me to come out of the house. When he became twelve, he was allowed to sit in the seat and pretend to steer. At fourteen I said he could start the car but not move it. Now he is driving. Have I contradicted myself simply because I was updating the message? There is no message contradiction simply because Jesus raises the bar of ethical conduct in the New Testament. Those who say there are message contradictions in the Bible reveal a surface understanding of God's Word. If you hear of a supposed contradiction and you don't have the answer, admit it and get some help. But don't be cowered into apathy about God's book when you don't always have the answer on the tip of your tongue.

2. *Supposed contradictions of numbers.* People say, "In

Mark and Luke it says that two blind men were healed at Jericho, and in Matthew it says that one blind man was healed at Jericho. That's a contradiction." Now hang on for a second. Is that a contradiction? A contradiction is when separate accounts of the same incident cannot be reconciled. Matthew doesn't say that two blind men weren't healed; he just says that one was. Now if two blind people were healed, and one of the writers of Scripture chooses to focus in on one of the accounts (which he actually does), is that a contradiction? Not at all! Beyond that, in the Gospel of John we are told that the books of all the world could not contain the things that Jesus did (John 21:25). It is very easy for me to conceive that Jesus healed the blind on several occasions in Jericho. One time He healed two people, and one time He healed one. Maybe the gospel writers are describing completely different events. These are not contradictions.

3. *Supposed parallel story contradictions.* Parallel stories occur when two or more places in the Bible describe the same event. Some people think that if the authors tell it differently, that's a contradiction. For instance, "Hey, in Genesis 1 it says that God created man and woman. In Genesis 2 it says He created man, and later on He created woman out of man." Like the guy who wrote Genesis

didn't figure that out himself! That is such a poor example of a contradiction. Clearly what we are getting in Genesis 1 is a flyby. "Creation. It goes like this: Hey, day one, two, three, four, five, six, rested on seven—that's chapter 1." Now for chapter 2 we are going to land the plane and focus in on the chief part of God's creation, man and woman. Let me tell you how that happened in more detail." There is no contradictory information in chapter 2—just more detail. Yet that easily resolved "apparent discrepancy" is one of the most common accusations leveled against the Bible.

Here's another one. This is supposed to be one of the major contradictions in the whole New Testament. Somebody who really wants to attack the Bible will say something like: "Hang on for a second. In Matthew 27, it says that Judas hanged himself. In Acts 1 it says that he fell headlong and burst open." Again the explanation is not very difficult. Judas hung himself on a tree in the Valley of Hinnom. If you have ever been there or seen pictures of this place, there are many rocky ledges surrounding the valley. No doubt what he did was go to the edge of a cliff, hang himself on a tree, and swing there for a period of time. At some point possibly the branch broke, and he fell to the valley below, landing on the jagged rocks that rise as high as twenty-five feet in the air. No doubt his body burst open at that point. Did he die on the tree, or did he botch the job of hanging himself and then die on the rocks? The Bible doesn't say where he died — only that he hung himself and burst open. One passage describes what Judas attempted to do and the other how he was found. Now that is not a contradiction! Yet those who know very little about the Bible raise these kinds of foolish issues in an attempt to discredit the only book God wrote and thereby undermine the faith of many. Don't let your faith be hurt by such attacks.

4. *Supposed historical contradictions.* In the past liberal scholars argued that there was no such place as Jericho — until it was found.[19] They argued that King David never lived — until they found an artifact with his name inscribed on it.[20] They argued that the Exodus from Egypt never occurred — but now some archaeological proof has been found.[21] Do you see a pattern developing here? Someone living today begins to think that he knows more about the times of the Bible than the people who wrote the Bible. Eventually, as more archaeological work is done, these critics are proved wrong, and the Bible is found to have been correct all along.

5. *Supposed scientific contradictions.* Did you ever have a science teacher who tried to jam the Bible? Some

high school teacher with a Bachelor's degree in science preys upon a teenager's faith with arguments so weak it would be laughable if it weren't so tragic. Joshua tells the story of the day when the sun stood still (Joshua 10:13). Now science knows that if the sun ever stood still, the earth would blow apart. Whoa! Like a God who could put one hand on the sun and hold it still couldn't put the other hand on the earth and hold it together too. These kinds of arguments reflect a blatant anti-supernaturalism that denies anything and everything that is not scientifically verifiable. I believe there is a God who spoke the universe into existence.[?] Everything in the Bible flows from that conviction. If you don't believe in a miracle-working God, then say so, but don't attack the Bible as ridiculous or contradictory simply because you have no faith in God.

Fulfilled Prophecy

One of the greatest proofs for the reliability of the Bible to me is the fact that the Old Testament is filled with prophecies that have come true.

• Isaiah 9:6-7 says that the Promised One would be born as a child and would establish an eternal kingdom.

• Isaiah 7:14 says that the Promised One would be born of a virgin.

• Psalm 72:9-11, 15 says that the Promised One would be worshiped by shepherds and kings, who would bring gifts of gold to Him.

• Micah 5:2 says that the Promised One would be born in Bethlehem.

Are those just lucky guesses? Coincidences, as some would say? Yeah, right! It's a coincidence that thousands of years before the birth of Jesus all of these prophecies were given and then fulfilled to the letter that very first Christmas. I'd like to see the Vegas odds on that.

There are sixty-one major prophecies concerning the life of Jesus Christ, written many hundreds of years before His birth.[23] Even unbelieving scientists applying the measurement of statistical probability tell us that the chances of just eight of those prophecies being fulfilled is one in 10^{17} (one hundred thousand trillion). This wasn't luck. Do you want to know what kind of a coincidence all of this would be? Take the whole state of Texas and cover it all with silver dollars two feet deep. Take a blindfolded person, tell him to wade out into the money, and pick up the silver dollar that has the red dot on it. That is the likelihood of all of the prophecies in the

Old Testament regarding Christ coming true by way of coincidence.[24]

EXPERIENTIAL EVIDENCE

People who have not read the Bible think that it is old and outdated and irrelevant, and I understand why. They think the Bible is like a book on parenting from the 1960s or a car repair manual from the 1920s. Experiential evidence deals with the effect the Bible can have on people's lives if they approach it sincerely. Have you ever approached it that way? Here are four evidences you could experience if you would come to the Bible with an open heart and mind:

1. *The Bible is gripping.* **Hebrews 4:12 (ESV) says, "For the word of God is living and active, sharper than any two-edged sword, piercing to the division of soul and of spirit, of joints and of marrow, and discerning the thoughts and intentions of the heart."** The Bible discerns what you are thinking and feeling. When you pick it up with a genuine desire to hear from God, it will grip you.

By God's grace I have a radio ministry that communicates God's Word on more than 1,000 stations around the country on a daily basis. When we began the ministry, I would never have believed the incredible impact it would have in people's lives. I have seen criminals, gripped by the Word of God, transformed and set free spiritually and emotionally while still within prison walls. Marriages so far gone that the people were already divorced have been put back together and brought to a place of total harmony, simply as the couple believed and obeyed the message of God's Word. I could tell countless stories of addiction broken, depression lifted, bodies healed, and families restored—all the result of people being gripped by the Word of God. Have you been gripped by it? Have you opened your heart and allowed its truths to penetrate your life and change you? If you do, you will have some experiential evidence of your own.

2. *The Bible is comforting.* As a pastor, I am continuously struck by the incredible comfort people find in the Word of God. I visit in hospitals with people facing very difficult surgery and stand with women who have lost their husbands or with parents who have lost children, and I hear these people tell of the comfort, strength, and peace beyond comprehension they find in God's Word. This isn't just a book that men wrote. Only God could write a book of such comfort.

3. *The Bible is convicting.* When someone stands up— even someone like me who is not especially smart—and opens God's book and begins to tell the things that are in it, the words penetrate people's hearts. I stand in the

pulpit nearly every weekend and see people with tears streaming down their cheeks as they hear God's Word. I see people under the penetrating power of the Holy Spirit, who can hardly even look up because God has taken His Word, and He is convicting their hearts. The Bible is convicting because it is God's book, and He uses its message to convict people.

4. Lastly, *the Bible is freeing*. Jesus said, **"You will know the truth, and the truth will make you free" (John 8:32)**. What a thrill it is not only to experience this freedom yourself, but then also to see others set free from sin and addictions and debilitating patterns of behavior, experiencing the freedom that God's truth brings. If this moment you are struggling under the weight of some burden you can't shake or some behavior you can't break, I commend to you the liberating message of the Bible. It will transform your life from the inside out.

Up Ahead

Maybe you have other questions about the Bible. Far more could be given in the way of evidence. Next we will look at the actual assembly of God's Word. Maybe you or someone you know has been asking: "How did all those little books become one big book?" Turn the page to find the answer.

2

WHERE DID THE BIBLE COME FROM?

Heaven and earth will pass away, but My words will not pass away.

MATTHEW 24:35

In the last chapter we looked at some evidence for the Bible as a supernatural book that God has produced and preserved. We went through external evidence, internal evidence, and then finally experiential evidence that God did in fact write a book.

But did you ever wonder where the Bible came from? How did we get the actual book that we hold in our hands? Did some guy say, "Hey, Martha. Hold my calls. I'm going up to my bedroom to write me some of that there Bible stuff"? Did God get a bunch of people together and do a group project, like a "Create the Bible

Weekend"? Most people have no idea how each Bible portion was written and gathered into the whole. Here are a few more questions I've heard people ask:

Did the people who were writing the Bible know that they were writing Scripture? Did they have any awareness that God was writing through them? Did they say to themselves, "People are going to be reading this for thousands of years"? Did some people try to write the Bible and fail? Or did they get it right the first time? Were they on a direct feed from almighty God? Or were they like, "Hey, God, I'm not getting this part—can we go over it again?"

The answers to these questions are extremely important. By studying the history of what did happen, we can greatly amplify our confidence in God's Word.

Amazingly, the Bible was written over 1,500 years by forty different authors on three different continents: Asia, Europe, and Africa. The classic New Testament passage on the Bible's origin is found in **2 Timothy 3:16**. But before we get there, let's back up to verse 15, which says, **"From childhood you have known the sacred writings which are able to give you the wisdom that leads to salvation through faith which is in Christ Jesus."**

I like that phrase at the end of the verse that says essentially, "Timothy, ever since you were a kid, you've known the Holy Scriptures, which are able to make you wise unto salvation." A lot of times people wonder, "How does a person come to be saved? How does a person come to know the Lord in a way that gets beyond religion to a genuine relationship?" Here we learn that the key is the Word of God. It is Scripture that penetrates people's hearts and allows them to comprehend the "wisdom that leads to salvation."

I praise God that in my family I'm a fourth-generation Christian. I was named after my great-grandfather's brother, James MacDonald. He was a man who was very effective at sharing his faith. In fact, my great-grand-father came to know Christ through his brother, my namesake. My great-grandfather's name was Hugh, and every year for many years, James would say to Hugh on his birthday, "Well, Hugh, you're a year older, but are you a year wiser? And are you yet wise to the ways of salvation?" After hearing this countless times, the truth finally penetrated his heart, and my great-grandfather received Christ into his life. Let me ask you that same question: "Are you wise to the ways of salvation?" (More on that in chapter 5.)

Either way, that kind of wisdom, salvation wisdom, can only come from God's Word, the book that our Creator has written. Now maybe you're thinking, *Hold on. Do you really believe that God sat at a desk and took a pen in His hand?* Well, not exactly like that. Back to 2 Timothy 3:15. The phrase "sacred writings" in verse 15 is composed of two Greek words, *hiera grammata,* which refer to the Old Testament Scriptures. Then in verse 16, "all Scripture" (Greek *pasa graphe*) was the term used in the early church to describe God's new writings.

Now notice what Paul says in verse 16: **"All Scripture is inspired by God."** All of it — the old and the new are both inspired, not just the part of the Bible that speaks to you. Not just the part that agrees with human wisdom. Not only the parts that bring you comfort. *All* Scripture — all of it — is given by inspiration of God. All sixty-six books. All 1,189 chapters. All 41,173 verses. All 3,566,480 letters. (It took me a long time to count that.)[1] All of it! The reason this is so important is that there are some parts of God's Word that we don't necessarily like or agree with. True or false? Some parts make us very uncomfortable because they convict us about our behavior and contradict views that we have thought to be correct. For that reason it is essential that we understand and accept the Bible's own assertion that *all* of it — the parts that bless me and the parts that stretch me — *all of it* is God's Word.

Notice the word *inspired* in 2 Timothy 3:16. Some versions say *inspiration.* The word *inspiration* translates a compound word in the original, *theopneustos.* It's a two-part word that means *God-breathed*. Once you understand the concept that all Scripture is inspired or God-breathed, you will never look at the Bible the same way again.

The best illustration I've heard to explain the concept of God-breathed is that of a sailboat. If you've ever been sailing, you know how incredible it is when the wind blows down, catches the sail, and carries the boat across the lake. The boat can't go where the wind won't take it.

In the same sense, God breathed the words of Scripture into the human authors. Yes, there were men who wrote it down. But the words that were written were the very words of God. God breathed or blew His words into the hearts and minds of the human sails. The end result is that what we have recorded in the Bible are the very words of God.

You say, "Can you be more specific?" Yes, I can. Not only did God write a book, but the Holy Spirit communicated the words. With so many people attacking and denying the true authorship of Scripture, you have to be very specific about what you mean when you say that the Bible is God's Word. Charles Ryrie, a professor at Dallas Theological Seminary, illustrates how times have changed:

> . . . Not many years ago, all you had to say to affirm your belief in the inspiration of the Bible was that you believed the Bible was the Word of God. That was it.

But as people have sliced and diced and criticized and hacked the Bible to bits [or *tried to*—obviously they've failed], it became necessary to add that you believed the Bible was the *inspired* Word of God. Later you had to include the *verbally* inspired Word of God. Then to mean the same thing, you had to say the plenary, verbally inspired Word of God. Today one has to say the plenary, verbally inspired, *infallible* Word of God. So many people have tried to undermine God's Word that you have to be really clear about what you mean.[2]

Let me touch on a couple of those things. We believe in the *plenary* inspiration of Scripture. We believe God wrote the whole thing from Genesis 1:1 to Revelation 22:21. We believe that God wrote it all and not just certain parts.

Secondly, we believe in the *verbal* inspiration of Scripture—not just that God chose the concepts, but that He chose the specific words. It wasn't like God was a coach as the apostles were writing down the New Testament—where He would say, "Hey, now write something about the feeding of the 5,000." God wasn't looking over the writer's shoulder and saying, "Good, yeah, that's really good. Now write something about how much I love them. Yeah, yeah, that's fantastic!" No, it wasn't like that at all. The Holy Spirit communicated the specific words—not just the paragraph headings.

You say, "Well, okay. But weren't the apostles writing many years *after* Christ lived? How can I be sure that the words they wrote down were actually the exact words that Jesus spoke? I can't remember what my mom said on the phone yesterday. How could they remember what Jesus said twenty, maybe even thirty years earlier?" First of all, I'm sure some of the disciples must have been saying, "Hey, is anybody getting this down? Lord, hang on for a second. Somebody grab a pencil. We've gotta get some of this stuff down."

But beyond that, Jesus promised the disciples help in remembering what He said. In **John 14:26** Jesus promised, **"The Holy Spirit, whom the Father will send in My name, He will teach you all things, and bring to your remembrance all that I said to you."** Isn't that a great pledge? So Jesus was like, "Hey. Don't worry about trying to remember every single thing I say. When it comes time to write the Gospels, when it comes time to write down the record of My life, I will have sent the Holy Spirit to indwell you, and He will bring to your mind all the words that I am speaking now." Wow! That is so great!

Look at John 16:12. Not only would the Holy Spirit bring to mind the things the disciples might tend to forget, but Jesus said, "There's a whole bunch of stuff

I *want* to tell you guys, but you can't handle it right now!" **John 16:12-13 says, "I have many more things to say to you, but you cannot bear them now. But when He, the Spirit of truth, comes, He will guide you into all the truth; for He will not speak on His own initiative, but whatever He hears, He will speak."** So some of what the apostles wrote down in the New Testament were things that Jesus had never even spoken. The Holy Spirit was adding things under the direction of God the Father. Notice that the disciples were promised additional insight from the Holy Spirit, who would be directly involved in the inspiration and recording of Scripture.

As these truths begin to dawn upon our understanding, we can see that almighty God is very deeply invested in this book called the Bible. He could have communicated with us in a lot of different ways. He could have written His message in the sky. He could have sent us all heavenly telegrams. He could have appeared in person annually to make His will known. There are many approaches God could have used to get His information to us. What God *chose to do* was to write a book. That *was* His plan, and that *is* His plan. He chose to make Himself and His will for us known in a book.

For this reason we need to be very sure that we do

not allow the words of the Bible to be diluted or compromised. They are not to be added to, subtracted from, or edited in any way. The words are not to be updated, amplified, or adjusted, not even once. In **Revelation 22:19,** almost the last verse in the Bible, it says, **"If anyone takes away from the words of the book of this prophecy, God will take away his part from the tree of life and from the holy city."**

Notice it says that if anyone takes away from the *words* of this book—not the concepts, not the thoughts, but the words. God doesn't want people messing with His book. He doesn't want people changing it. He doesn't want people arrogantly thinking they can upgrade it or make it more accessible or less offensive or whatever. But there are some very troubling trends in the world today related to people taking God's Word seriously.

First, I am concerned about the emphasis on study notes over the sacred text. It really bothers me to turn through the pages of a Bible and see the study notes written in the same font right alongside God's Word. Some people spend more time reading the notes than what God actually wrote. There is danger in giving the words of men an authority parallel to the words of God. When you pick up a Bible, make sure you're learning *the Bible,* and not just a single person's thoughts about this book.[3] People have been understanding God's Word without notes for thousands of years. Surely the most educated group of people who ever lived don't need someone to interpret every single word.

Here's a second trend that concerns me: marketing the Bible by creating a special version for every demographic segment of society — the High School Bible, the College Bible, the Worship Bible, the Seeker Bible, the Revival Bible, the Seniors' Bible, the Little Kids' Bible. It's out of control! Where did this idea come from? From people who want to get God's life-changing truth into the hands of everyone, or from those who want to profit from the Word of God through marketing techniques? Next we're going to have the Farmer's Bible, but we'll need a Crop Farmer's Bible because his needs are a lot different from those of a livestock farmer! The livestock farmer will have to have his own Bible. Ridiculous!

The third and most dangerous trend in our day is a dramatic shift in the actual philosophy of translation itself. For 2,000 years people translated the New Testament with one primary agenda: *accuracy*. They tolerated translations that were awkward or even unclear at times because they believed that the Holy Spirit gave the precise words that God the Father wanted, and their greatest passion was to know exactly what God said. But nowadays people say, "Just make it readable. People will never understand *that*; smooth it over, fill in the gaps, and make sure no one is left pondering what it means." Many of today's translators have forgotten that God's Word cannot be known apart from the work of the Holy Spirit (1 Corinthians 2:14). If the Spirit of God is opening the heart of a person, he or she will understand God's Word. If the Spirit of God is not guiding them into truth (cf. John 16:13), no amount of "dumbing down" the Bible and injuring its accuracy will help. Good modern translations that present the greatest possible word-for-word accuracy would be the New American Standard Bible and the English Standard Version.

If we accept the biblical truth that God chose the words, then clearly we should not be tampering with those words in any way. But if the exact words don't matter, maybe I should release the "Gen-X Bible" I have been working on. Here's a sample from **Luke 15:14**, the story of the Prodigal Son. The English Standard Version says, **"And when he had spent everything, a severe famine arose in that country, and he began to be in need."** That's an accurate translation. Now here's my Gen-X version: "So the dude looks in his bag for a bit more green, and it's like bone-dry. To make it worse, there's like no food anywhere—not even a can of bean dip or something. And you know how bad you can get the munchies if you've been partying. So this guy is completely bent over with a hunger problem, and his formerly full pockets are way empty."[4]

Is that where we want to go with the Bible? Many people are headed in that direction. We need those who will stand up for *verbal* inspiration. Some people say, "But, Lord, we're helping people understand Your Word." God's like, "Whew! I couldn't have done it without you." Remember: God wrote a book! The Holy Spirit communicated the words, and the words matter! God can handle the obvious limitations of language equivalency if we do our best to render word-for-word accuracy in our translations.

That's God's part. Now let's consider the human role in the writing of Scripture. The apostles wrote the words down. This is where a lot of people begin to struggle, saying, "I don't have a problem with God's book. As long as it's in God's hands, I feel really confident about it. It's when some guy is actually writing it down—that's what troubles me. It's like, what if they got distracted or forgot a part or something? I forget stuff all the time. How can I be sure that they didn't mess up the Bible somehow?"

The other key New Testament passage on where the

Bible came from is **2 Peter 1:20-21: "But know this first of all, that no prophecy of Scripture is a matter of one's own interpretation, for no prophecy was ever made by an act of human will, but men moved by the Holy Spirit spoke from God."**

Notice first of all the phrase, "for no prophecy was ever made by an act of human will." While it was not man's will creating the Scriptures, God did work through the authors' individual personalities. God did not simply dictate the Bible. It wasn't like John said, "Okay, now let's do chapter 3, verse 16. 'For' — Okay, got it. What's next? — 'God' — Got it. Next? — 'so' — Got it. — 'loved' — Got it. — 'the' — Next? — 'world' — Great!" The apostles and other authors of Scripture had more than a secretarial function. We believe that God supernaturally flowed His word-for-word truth through the personality and mind of the author. If you look at the life of Peter, for example, he was excitable, enthusiastic, and very verbal. When you read his writings, they are the same way. He is talking about this, and then he's talking about that, and next he's changing the subject a third time. He's all over the place, and you can see Peter's personality in the way he writes. Or you might say, in the way God writes through him.

Now take the apostle Paul. He was like a lawyer:

Point one, point two, point three. Perfect logic. Flawless argumentation. That's how Paul writes. John was the one who leaned on Jesus' bosom at the Last Supper. John was tenderhearted and loving. You can see his personality in the Gospel and Epistles God wrote through him. John constantly brings up God's love and the way we must love each other. Do you see how God worked through the individuality of the human authors to bring the truth He wanted to communicate? It was God's content delivered through human personality.

But not just any old human personality. I don't think many of us would have been qualified to write the Bible. I know I wouldn't have been. God chose some of the most righteous, godly people who have ever lived as the instruments to write His book. They were apostles and prophets—pure vessels, clear channels. They were men with the capacity to hear God very directly and perfectly. These were men who had a lifetime of experience in downloading God's heart to people.[5]

Now we're trying to answer the question: Where did the Bible come from? And hopefully you get the God part and the human part. Next let's consider the *book* part. Maybe you think to yourself, *A period of 1,500 years, forty different authors, sixty-six books. I can't find a book that*

I read last year. How did sixty-six little books written over 1.5 millennia get together in one big book?

To state it simply, the early church pulled it all together. Very early, within a very few years, the leaders of the church put these sixty-six books together, concluding, "These are the books God has written." Again, while most people have little or no knowledge of how this happened, a clear understanding of the historical record can do a lot to bolster faith in God's Word. The process they used involved two main steps: 1) eliminating the inferior writings; and 2) identifying the inspired writings.

ELIMINATING THE INFERIOR WRITINGS

The writing of the Scripture was complete by A.D. 95. Hundreds of manuscripts were copied and recopied so that everyone could hear the messages God had given. But there were also many writings that were not inspired by the Holy Spirit. So it wasn't as if these sixty-six books were off in a pile all by themselves. Around and among the writings that would eventually be recognized as God's Word were others that were of mere human origin.

Canonization is the word that is used to describe how the individual books of Scripture were set apart and recognized. The word *canon* actually means "measuring rod." So the canon of Scripture is the collection of books that measured up. Norman Geisler and William Nix have written *A General Introduction to the Bible*,[6] in which they explain the process of canonization.

There were four categories into which the available religious writings were placed, and the first category was called the *homolegomena*, which means "one word" or "agreement." These books were accepted by everyone and recognized quickly.

Then there was the second group called the *antilegomena*. These were books that were initially spoken against. People said, "We're not sure about this one. Should it really be in the Bible?" There were five Old Testament *antilegomena* books. People weren't sure about the Song of Solomon at first because they thought it was too sensual. Ecclesiastes was also doubted initially because people thought it was too cynical. The book of Esther was questioned because it never mentions the name of God, though as people studied Esther, they came to see the thread of God's sovereignty woven beautifully through its story. The other two doubtful books were Proverbs and Ezekiel.

The New Testament books initially included in the *antilegomena* were Hebrews, James, 2 Peter, 2 and 3 John, Jude, and Revelation. Most of these were initially doubted on the grounds of authorship. For example, until the early church fathers were convinced that John really wrote 2 and 3 John, they weren't willing to say that it was God's Word. All of these were initially questioned but were eventually recognized as sacred Scripture.

A third category of writings you've probably heard of is the *apocryphal* books. The word *apocrypha* means "hidden" or "hard to understand." These were also in the pile of books that were examined and measured against the standard of God's authorship. There were fourteen to fifteen apocryphal books. A battle continues over these books in that the Roman Catholic church did not fully recognize them until the middle of the second millennium. Several apocryphal books were added to the Bible during the time of the Protestant Reformation when certain Christians were questioning specific doctrines of the Catholic church and objecting to the lack of biblical support for such teaching. These apocryphal books, which do not agree with the originally canonized books, are used to substantiate Catholic teachings such as purgatory and prayers for the dead. These later books have always been noticeably inferior, and by virtue of their contradictions of teachings of the books originally recognized, apocryphal books should not be considered books that God wrote.

The last category of writings considered during the process of canonization was the *pseudepigrapha*. This grouping, though it includes possibly 300 or more writings, focused in on 18 specific ones that, while high in quality, were unanimously recognized as clearly not God's Word. These books were filled with fanciful, magical kinds of things such as stories about Jesus when He was a little boy and how He would do tricks for His friends. Everyone agreed that these were the creations of people's imagination rather than messages given supernaturally by God.

IDENTIFYING THE INSPIRED WRITINGS

I remember when I studied these matters for the first time, I had one burning question. You may be asking that question even now: "What specific standards did they actually use to establish the canon?" In reality there were five tests the writings had to pass in order to be considered God's Word. We can call them "five proofs of inspiration."

1. *Authority.* The book under consideration had to have authority. If you have ever studied God's Word with an open heart, you know firsthand that it is unlike anything else you have ever read. The Bible has an almost measurable aura of authority. This authority was also present in the teaching of Jesus and was read-

ily apparent to His audience. **"They were amazed at His teaching; for He was teaching them as one having authority" (Mark 1:22).** Although we live in a day that repudiates authority, the early church understood that anything truly written by God would need to have an obvious ring of authority.

If you were to read through the whole Bible and circle every time it says, "And God said," and "Thus says the Lord," and "The word of the Lord came to," you would discover that more than 4,000 times the writers of Scripture say without embarrassment or apology that what they are saying and writing is the very Word of God. For this reason the early church knew that if the specific writing under consideration was in fact God's Word, then all would agree that it communicated a sense of divine authority.

2. *Authorship.* Was it written by a man of God? Was it written by an apostle or one of their close associates (e.g., Mark, Luke)? It may have been that some were claiming that certain books were written by apostles when in fact they were not. Others were doubting truly apostolic writings simply because the subject matter or the circumstances of writing caused the apostle to write in a way that seemed different from other things he had written. Before a book could be accepted as from God,

the early church wanted to be sure who the author was and that he had the credentials of one through whom God would choose to give His Word. As I mentioned above, this is why some books were initially disputed. When the authorship issue was settled, the matter was settled, and the books were included in the Scripture

3. *Authenticity.* Does the book tell the truth about God and man? Does the book tell the truth about salvation? Is it consistent with the rest of what we know to be God's Word? This cross-checking is why there are no contradictions in the Bible, by the way. We like to think that we're the smartest people who ever lived, but in reality we do not have a greater intelligence—not by a long shot. In fact, I'd like to suggest to you that the people who were living on the earth during the canonization of Scripture were extremely intelligent. Instead of wasting their lives watching television, they spent many, many years poring over the text—every word, every line, every verse, every chapter, comparing with other Scriptures back and forth, back and forth, and then confirming, "This is God's Word because it agrees one hundred percent with everything else we know." They would take a particular verse and compare it to the Pentateuch written by Moses. Then they would compare it to the books of each of the prophets. Then they would

line the writing up with Psalms and other Old Testament books of poetry. They demanded that the message be consistent in every detail, or else it was not authentic. This is why the Apocrypha never passed the early test and was never accepted.

4. *Alive.* **Hebrews 4:12** says that **"the word of God is *living* and active."** It's powerful. It changes people's lives. As these books were circulated, one of the things that people wanted to know was, "Is this powerful? Is this life-changing truth? Does this impact our lives?" Surely a message given by God Himself will have powerful results in the lives of those who read it. If it does, then that book was more likely to be confirmed as the Word of God.

5. *Acceptance.* This was the most important test of all. Did the other churches receive it as God's Word? You can imagine as the letter to the Romans was written, it was passed around to this church and then circulated to a second church, then a third, and a fourth, and so on. As the people of God in each community read it, did they confirm and recognize that it was in fact the very Word of God, or was it simply a human communication? Were the churches unanimous in their perception of the book? **First Thessalonians 2:13** records an actual occurrence of this process happening in an informal way when Paul

reports: **"For this reason we also constantly thank God that when you received the word of God which you heard from us, you accepted it not as the word of men, but for what it really is, the word of God, which also performs its work in you who believe."** The strongest test of the writings was their rejection or acceptance as God's Word by the individual churches and their elders.

So that's where the Bible came from. God wrote a book. The Holy Spirit communicated the words. Men wrote them down. The early church pulled the writings together.

Do you believe that God wrote a book? Because if you do, then that book should be getting a lot of attention from you, shouldn't it? If God really did write a book, we ought to be reading it, studying it, memorizing it, and letting it guide our lives. Go to the next page and learn exactly what the Bible can do for you and your family.

3

WHAT IS THE BIBLE GOOD FOR?

For you have exalted above all things your name and your word.

PSALM 138:2b ESV

Now to this point you have read and hopefully answered two very important questions: Why do we believe the Bible is God's Word, and where did the Bible come from? But maybe the real question you have been wrestling with is, why all the fuss? Who cares about the Bible anyway? What's the big deal? Why does it matter? At the root of these kinds of questions is this basic inquiry: What is the Bible good for? The people I talk to aren't interested so much in what something is; they want to know what it can do to help them. To say it another way, they want to know if the Bible will make a practical difference in their lives, if it will change them for the better. It may surprise you to know that God's Word is not only open to that question; it is up for it. God's Word has never been tried and found lacking; it has only been found difficult and therefore not tried. In this chapter I want to cover with you the incredible promises the Bible makes about itself and give examples of how those promises are being faithfully fulfilled in people's lives all over our world today. I am going to explain just a few of the countless benefits that could be yours if you would daily open and read the book that God has written.

Let's Define Our Terms

Have you ever heard someone say, "The Bible has all the answers," or "The Bible has all the information people need to live their lives"? Those kinds of categorical statements seem far-fetched to me. Is the Bible a book about science? Does it teach us how to fix our cars or balance our budgets? It's not a cookbook, right? Does the Bible supercede studies of anthropology, psychology, and sociology? I mean, what kind of book is this exactly? What do people mean when they say that the Bible is sufficient to solve the problems facing our postmodern world? And isn't it possible that people are claiming more for the Bible than it actually claims for itself? Let's use the following statement to summarize what the Bible *is* good for, and then after I explain it briefly, we will discuss the Bible's practicality for you and your loves ones. Here it is:

The Bible is one hundred percent accurate in all that it asserts and constitutes all truth essential for human happiness.

In a few places the Bible contradicts the current findings of the social science profession (I say "current" because the social sciences seem to change their presuppositions as often as most of us change our underwear). In those instances I trust the Bible and wait for these supposed sciences to figure out they are wrong.[1] Countless times skeptics have asserted, "Here it is. I've finally figured it out. I've found a place where I can prove the Bible to be false." Then years later they say, "Oops!" The further I go in my own lifetime of learning, the more I see the benefits of avoiding the shifting sands of current scholarship. I encourage you to rest instead on the solid ground of believing the Bible to be one hundred percent accurate in all that it asserts.

WHAT ABOUT ALL THE STUFF THE BIBLE NEVER MENTIONS?

Now I am not saying that all truth is in God's Word. There are many true things not recorded in the Bible.

For example, the mathematic equation 2 + 2 = 4 is not anywhere in the Bible. Yes, there are countless matters about which the Bible is totally silent. That is why I used the word *essential*. We have never discovered or learned a single piece of information outside the Bible that is essential for human happiness. Oh, we have learned some helpful things maybe — if you plant your tulips this way, they'll grow bigger. Very helpful, thank you, but not essential. Or sparks and tinder make fire that is useful in a thousand different ways. Notice, useful but not essential to human happiness. Every piece of information *essential to human happiness* is in God's Word because God loves you. He doesn't want you to be without anything that you need to experience life to its fullest.

To state that the Bible is not missing anything essential to human happiness is quite an assertion. Am I claiming more for the Bible than it claims for itself? That's the question we're going to answer in this chapter.

THE BIBLE'S CLAIMS

Take a moment and read **Psalm 19:7-11 (NKJV).**

> **The law of the LORD is perfect, converting the soul; the testimony of the LORD is sure, making wise the simple. The statutes of the LORD are right, rejoic-**

ing the heart; the commandment of the LORD is pure, enlightening the eyes; the fear of the LORD is clean, enduring forever; the judgments of the LORD are true and righteous altogether. More to be desired are they than gold, yea, than much fine gold; sweeter also than honey and the honeycomb. Moreover by them Your servant is warned, and in keeping them there is great reward.

Wow! What you have just read is one of the greatest statements on the sufficiency of God's Word in the whole Bible. In fact, I believe it is second only to Psalm 119, which has 176 verses on the subject. But Psalm 19:7-11 is the Scripture that most concisely and specifically relates the value of the Bible. It is God's own statement about what the Bible is "good for."[2]

Notice that in verses 7-10 there are five names for the Scriptures: law, testimony, precepts, commandment, and judgments. Each is a synonym for God's Word, specifically attributing to Scripture a slightly different dimension. It's not unlike the way we might break down the components of our home into master bedroom, kitchen, bathroom, family room, etc. Each description gives details under the broader heading of "home."

Next we observe six adjectives that describe the particular terms for God's Word: perfect, sure, right, pure, clean, and true.

Finally, if you look closely, you'll see six results or consequences that follow for the person who takes God's Word to heart. Notice that the Bible restores the soul, makes wise the simple, rejoices the heart, enlightens the eyes, endures forever, and is true and altogether righteous. Putting together all these terms for God's Word with six adjectives and six results, we have six strong statements about the impact God's Word can make in your life. Let's look at each one more closely with the goal of accurately assessing what the Bible itself claims it is good for.

GOD'S WORD TRANSFORMS US

That assertion flows from **Psalm 19:7a (NKJV)**, which says, **"The law of the LORD is perfect, converting the soul."** Let's walk through it a word at a time. The word *law* means the Torah, "the law for life, rule for living." When God's Word is spoken of as law, it means the norm or the standard by which every action is measured. I love that phrase, "the law of the Lord." Whose law is it? The Bible is the law "of the Lord." Now for centuries men have laid down their laws—some wise, some foolish, always inevitably contradictory, seldom justly administered, always changing. These are the laws of men. But that's the great thing about God's law; it's not the law of men, but the law of the Lord. How is it described? The law of the Lord "is perfect." That's what God says about His own Word. The word *perfect* means literally "all-sided" or "many faceted." It means "all encompassing" or "thorough in every respect." In fact this "law of the Lord" is so comprehensive that we are told that it is effective in "converting the soul."

You have a soul and so do I. The soul is the part of a human being that thinks and feels and chooses and relates to God. Animals do not have souls. When animals die, they go down into the earth. But when people die, their souls go upward and give account to God (Ecclesiastes 3:21 NKJV). We all have souls. It's the immaterial part of every human being—the part of us that will live forever. God created us with souls so we could relate to others and to Him, but instead we have all chosen to sin, to go our own way. For that reason our souls are damaged and deserving of God's judgment.

Now what the Scripture is telling us is that God's Word is the answer to our soul problem. To paraphrase what is written: "God's law is so totally comprehensive that it is able to convert a soul." The word *convert* there is a fantastic word. Some translations use the English word *revive* or *restore*, but the more common meaning is "transform." How phenomenal to comprehend what

God is telling us about His Word. God promises that His law is so totally comprehensive that whatever the condition of the individual soul, His Word can transform it from top to bottom, from inside to outside, from past to future. Scripture changes you to the very core of who you are as a person.

Over a hundred years ago one of the greatest preachers who ever walked the face of this earth said these words: "The great means of the conversion of sinners is the Word of God, and the more closely we keep to it in our ministry, the more likely we are to be successful. It is God's Word rather than man's comment on God's Word which is made mighty with souls."[3] I could tell dramatic stories of drug addicts freed and prostitutes transformed, but here are a couple of stories I think most of us can relate to a little better.

Two Souls Transformed by God's Word

Our church meets in a massive furniture warehouse we bought several years ago and renovated into a place of worship. In fact, it had been several things before we bought it. First it was a furniture store. That eventually went under. Then it was one of those wholesale buying clubs, and that also went bankrupt a few years later. Finally this big old warehouse was used as a sort of

Home Depot wanna-be. This guy named Marty used to shop at the Home Base, as it was called, and bought all sorts of tools and materials for his building projects.

When I met him, he admitted that being a part-time "tool guy" was his whole identity, and his Sunday morning trips to buy home improvement stuff was like his religion. While he was upset when his "house of worship" went under, he was even more ticked off when he discovered it was going to be "made into some stupid church or something." In fact, he was so frustrated by what he considered a total waste of a perfectly good retail space that he got curious and came to check us out when the church opened its doors.

The first day he came, he had a pretty bad attitude. He sat in the front row with his wife, not interested, not wanting to be there, and angry that the church even existed. But over a period of several weeks the truth of God's Word began to penetrate his heart—so much so that he couldn't keep from coming back. Before too long Marty committed his life to Jesus Christ.

Here's a guy so filled with himself that his marriage was in deep weeds, and he wasn't much of a father either. He was totally consumed with his own problems until God's Word penetrated his heart and totally changed his life. In fact, he is so transformed that he stands up in front of the entire congregation at this church he used to hate and, with a smile from ear to ear, tells everyone present about the new joy he has found in following Christ and learning from the Bible. Beyond that, Marty is so excited about his faith that he shares God's truth with others, and they are beginning to see their lives transformed as well. God's Word can and often does overcome the resistance of a stubborn heart and change it forever.

I could tell hundreds of stories like that. I see them on a daily basis, but here's just one more illustration of how the law of the Lord converts the soul. Recently I was speaking at a banquet up in Wisconsin and heard a powerful story about the transforming power of God's Word from a couple at my table. John and Tina had been happily married for a number of years when John began to act in an unusual manner. His normal interest in family and church was eroding, and he began to be consumed with selfish thoughts and desires to run from the life he had built for himself. This struggle went on under the surface for a season but eventually burst forth in a great overflow of sinfulness. He left his wife and told his fourteen-year-old son that "he would have to be the man of the house."

John moved out of state and began to live in a way

that he himself describes as "running into sin, pleasure, adultery, pornography, growing worse in my dysfunctional thinking" by the day. The downward spiral continued to escalate until his credit ran out, and he began depleting his pension. The news of this breach of trust forced Tina to file for divorce to protect the financial security of her children. Yet even after the divorce was finalized, this loving wife kept praying and believing God for a miracle. On a human level it looked as if there was no hope that John would ever be turned around. Typically people in this kind of desperation scan the horizon for some hint of where a miracle could even come from. But I know from experience that God works the miracle most often through His Word.

Even though the situation looked grim, Tina began to listen to our Bible teaching on the radio, and the Lord convicted her that her divorce did not have to be the final chapter in this sad story. She continued praying for her former husband, who had moved back to the area and in with another woman. Tina would give him tapes of Bible teaching and especially teaching on what the Bible says about divorce. After a time the Word of God began to soften his heart, and he realized that the ache he was feeling inwardly could only be satisfied by turning from his sin and selfishness and realigning his life in obedience to Scripture. I say "realigning" because he had been a pastor for fifteen years before this collapse into misery. Amazingly, one who had given himself to reaching others with God's Word had walked away from that same message and done irreparable damage in the process. Or so it seemed.

Tina continued to persist in faithfully loving her ex-husband, and eventually John came to a place of sincere repentance. He allowed the Word of God to penetrate his distorted thinking and in an amazing series of transforming decisions was eventually fully reunited with his wife and kids. They were so fully reconciled, in fact, that John and Tina decided to be remarried. They came to the banquet that night to relay to me the incredible miracles of transformation they had experienced through the Word of God at work in their life. A miracle, no doubt about it, and another trophy to the amazing capacity of the law of the Lord in converting a soul.

To Be More Specific

Now maybe you're wondering what a converted soul actually looks like. If so, consider this second assertion about the value of Scripture: **"The testimony of the Lord is sure, making wise the simple" (Psalm 19:7b nkjv).** I love that word *testimony*, used only here in all the Psalms.

The root word means "to bear witness." "The testimony of the LORD" pictures God as giving witness to Himself. God is giving a report or, we might say, taking the stand in His own defense. It's as if almighty God is being sworn in at a trial, raising His right hand, and bearing witness to Himself. "I, God, do solemnly—" Well, God certainly doesn't need to take any oaths. In fact, the Bible says that God cannot lie (Titus 1:2), but the word *testimony* carries the idea of God bearing witness to Himself.

Note how the testimony is described: "The testimony of the LORD is sure." The word *sure* there conveys the idea of being "reliable" or "durable." It's actually similar to the verb that means "amen." You could translate it: "The testimony of the LORD is amen." Everything that God says is right on! This phrase pictures God as one who, in His Word, tells it like it is.

Now notice the result. God's witness to Himself is so reliable, so sure, that it makes the simple wise. The word translated "simple" literally means "openness," but that's not a compliment. The meaning here is more akin to the way we use the word *simpleton*—a person whose mind is like a house with the front and back doors always open. So stuff just comes in and out, and the simpleton has no ability to discern which thoughts are valuable and which are useless. Some thought or idea blows in the front door, and such persons are like, "I think I'll do this with my life now." Then, "Oh no, no, *this* seems like a better idea—that's the direction I'll head." The testimony of the Lord is *so* reliable that it is able to take people like that, with no clue about where they are headed or why, and turn them into persons of wisdom.

The fact is that we live in a world of simpletons—people who value what is worthless and disdain what is priceless. People who wink at perversity and wince at morality. Men and women who embrace what is foolish and reject true wisdom. You ask, "Is there any hope for this world?" Yes, there is—in God's book. The Scripture says that the testimonies of the Lord are sure, making wise the simple. Wisdom in Scripture carries the idea of being skilled at daily living. To the Greeks of biblical times, wisdom was to know, but to the Hebrews here in the Old Testament, wisdom was to do. In fact to them, the biggest fool of all was the person who knew but didn't do. The testimonies of the Lord are so reliable that they can take a vacillating simple person and make him or her skilled at daily living.

I remember the first time I met Luis. He was so angry and so intent on doing what he wanted with his life. Though he was destroying his family and himself, he couldn't see it. Luis was addicted to alcohol, and that addiction was like a malignant tumor in his heart. For months he and his family had been attending a church that neither preached nor really believed God's Word. Luis enjoyed the comfort of attending a church that never required him to face up to the fact that he was walking on the path of destruction.

His wife had heard through some friends about our church and had been praying for many weeks that somehow she could get her husband under the unapologetic preaching of God's Word, but he resolutely refused to come. Then one morning right out of the blue, he not only agreed to attend, but he actually suggested it. Astonished, his wife and family got into the car and came to our church and, incredibly, walked right down to the front row. Little did Luis realize it, but he was keeping an appointment with almighty God.

That morning I was teaching from God's Word on the subject "Wise Up About Alcohol." Luis squeaked and squirmed on the pew, but the Word of God got through to his heart. Later that week he gave his life to Jesus Christ, and by God's grace has not had a drink since that day. His marriage has been healed, his life has been transformed, and his children are filled with joy. Why? Because the testimony of the Lord is so reliable,

God's witness about Himself is so trustworthy, that it can take a stubborn, hardhearted alcoholic, with no discernment about right and wrong, and actually make him skilled in the matters of life and happiness.

HOW TO BE HAPPY

And even that's not all. **"The statutes of the LORD are right, rejoicing the heart" (Psalm 19:8a NKJV).** Notice the progression here. First the Word of God converts you. Then it makes you wise, and then it causes your heart to rejoice.

Statutes are God's rulings, His prescriptions, pronouncements, principles.

The world has principles, too, doesn't it? Stuff like: "You only go around once, so go for the gusto." I've heard that a lot. Or how about: "Fool me once, shame on you. Fool me twice, shame on me." Everyone has heard that worldly principle—sort of like: "You might mess with me once, but don't ever try it again." Right? I could list hundreds of such shortsighted stupidisms. You have your favorites, I'm sure.

But in contrast to all this faulty human thinking that seldom guides and never satisfies are the "statutes of the LORD." Let me tell you something about God's statutes. "The statutes of the LORD are right." Isn't that great to know? They're not off-track, not even off by a degree. They're one hundred percent right. God's principles, His statutes, are correct in all that they assert. They set a right path. Life is like a maze, and the statutes of God set a right path through the maze so that we don't wander aimlessly or get lost or sidetracked by things that don't ultimately matter. God's statutes take the pressure off.

Never do we have so much joy in this world as when we are living in conformity to God's Word. Never. Like an engine firing on all cylinders. Like a gazelle running full speed. Like a symphony — every instrument pounding out the melody and harmonies in perfect tune and rhythm.

I have very sensitive ears. The downside of sensitive ears is that disruptive noise (like the intercom on airplanes) makes me a bit crazy. The upside, however, is that I can hear every instrument and every subtlety in a piece of music. At church I drive our worship team nuts because I always know when an individual voice or instrument is out of tune. I know because I can hear it.

God's precepts give anyone who will listen the ability to hear when our lives are out of tune. When we consistently conform our behavior to God's Word, our conduct won't grate upon our ears, but instead will bring rejoicing to our hearts. Do you know what I'm talking about? When you're doing the things that God created you to do and told you to do in His Word, your life will begin to overflow with a joy that you never imagined was possible.

A good illustration of this principle comes from an encounter Jesus had with some of His disciples. After Jesus was crucified, they were bumming out major league, not knowing what to do next. As they were walking on the road to Emmaus, Jesus appeared and began walking with them, but they did not recognize Him. Luke records that as they walked, He **"expounded unto them in all the scriptures the things concerning himself" (Luke 24:27** KJV).

But all of a sudden they recognized him, and immediately Jesus vanished. Thinking back, they considered what they were feeling as the Lord explained and proclaimed the Scriptures to them: **"Did not our heart burn within us, while he talked with us by the way . . . ?" (Luke 24:32** KJV). Jesus was expounding all the Scriptures in the Old Testament that spoke about Himself.

There is a joy that comes to a human heart when it rightly understands the Bible. This joy cannot be experienced any other way. I like what it says in **Jeremiah**

15:16: **"Your words were found and I ate them, and Your words became for me a joy and the delight of my heart."**

Maybe as you sit or stand reading this book, you know deep within yourself that you are not experiencing that joy and happiness that your heart desires. Unfortunately, the things that we think will make us happy do not. Might I challenge you to turn off the television, unplug the phone, and give the book God has written a chance to feed and fill your soul, maybe like you have never known before. God's Word brings us joy. **"The statutes of the LORD are right, rejoicing the heart."**

KEEP THE CAMERAS ROLLING

I feel like we're in one of those infomercials right now. I am trying to show you the incredible benefits that can be yours if you dig into God's Word, and you may be ready to "call the toll-free number," but I keep saying, "And even that's not all." Well, stick with me. I may be in danger of overselling, but there are still three more benefits you can receive from God's book.

Number four is that God's Word dispels the darkness. **"The commandment of the LORD is pure, enlightening the eyes" (Psalm 19:8b NKJV).** Commandments are orders or divine decrees, the things God insists that we do and keep doing. I bet you already knew that the Bible is filled with commands. Not only does it give commands, but it also often lays out the negative consequences of disobedience and the positive results of doing what God requires. Now notice **Psalm 19:8b: "The commandment of the LORD is pure."** One version translates *pure* as "radiant." The idea there is the absence of impurity, the absence of a visual impediment. No blockage or blot of any kind. I love that truth because I love things that are clear.

Do you remember a few years back when a new beverage came out called "Clearly Canadian"? (Being a Canadian, I loved the name.) The product featured wonderful berry flavors with a sparkling, fresh taste, sold in a blue glass bottle. Just describing it to you makes me thirsty for that clear, crisp sensation I get in my mouth when I drink it. To me there is just something wonderful about stuff that is clear. When I buy something for my home, I search for things with the words on the package "no assembly required," because I hate those manuals that are so unclear and impossible to follow. I don't like my glasses to be dirty. I like clean windows and clear highways, and I when I get stressed out, I have to clear my calendar. No doubt about it, "clear" rocks! That's why I was so excited the day I understood for the first time that the Word of God is clear. You can pick it up yourself and understand it. The commandments of God are clear. People try to say that the Bible is confusing because they don't want to accept its message, but actually the Bible is incredibly clear in what it asserts — so much so that God promises it will enlighten our eyes.

Sad but true, the world we live in is very dark. All around us difficult, perplexing, painful things are happening to people, and, like a bunch of blind men, most people really have no idea why. If you ask them why there is so much suffering in the world, they will tell you it's God's fault or say that if there was a God, He would stop it. The reason they don't understand the world is because they have never seriously consulted the book that God has written to dispel all that darkness and confusion. If you are struggling this moment with a lot of questions about your life and the world we live in, if you struggle to reconcile what you see with the existence of a loving God, you really must get into the book where He explains all of that. If you do, without a doubt you will discover that **"the commandment of the LORD is pure, enlightening the eyes."**

Now let's just take a moment and review. We've learned that the law of the Lord is so comprehensive that it is able to totally transform the inner person. We've learned that God's testimony about Himself is so reliable that it can take a vacillating simpleton and make him or her skilled in daily living. We've learned that God's divine principles set a right path through the maze of life and cause our hearts to rejoice. Wow! What statements! We've learned that the commands of God are so crystal-clear that they bring light into the darkness in every human heart.

AND EVEN THAT'S NOT ALL

Here's the fifth thing: God's Word adds stability. **Psalm 19:9a (NKJV) says, "The fear of the LORD is clean, enduring forever."** Fear is the attitude of heart that seeks a right relationship to the fear source. When you have the fear of the Lord, you have something in your heart that makes you want to be in a right relationship with God. The fear of the Lord is like a wall around your behavior that hems you in and protects you from making bad choices. It's the fear of the Lord that causes you to avoid certain behaviors that would displease Him and bring negative consequences. If there are certain things you hope you will never do because you believe God might chasten or judge you harshly if you did them, then you have, to some degree, the fear of the Lord. The Bible is a book that instructs us on how to relate to God properly — that is, in the fear of the Lord.

It is interesting that the fear of the Lord is described

as clean. Scripture says in **Hebrews 10:31, "It is a terrifying thing to fall into the hands of the living God."** Yet into His hands we all *will* fall someday, and the Bible is the book that tells us how to get ready. If you fear God in this life, you will not have to fear Him in the life to come, because the fear of the Lord is clean. By that the Bible means that the fear of the Lord is "without blemish"; it is "undiminished, uncompromised, and without delusion or defilement" of any kind. The Word of God is full-strength from cover to cover. There is no part of God's Word that is of inferior quality or that would lead you astray in any respect. You can believe all of it because it is *clean.*

In fact, the Word is not only clean, but it endures forever. How badly we need a source of stability when circumstances shake our world. We never have to worry that God's Word may be out of date or in need of revision; it is just as relevant as it was the day it was written. Circumstances may change, cultures and world leaders may come and go, but God's Word is always current because it deals with two things that never change—the God who made us and the deepest needs of the human heart. You could walk away from God and His Word today, and if He spared your life by His grace, you could come back *fifty* years from now, and His book would be exactly the same—offering the exact same answers, setting you back on the exact same path. The Word of God is clean. It is full-strength. It is uncompromised, and it endures forever. In every place, in every generation, in every century, in every millennium the Bible is a source of stability for all who turn to it.

I will never forget the news conference of the Willis family after their van exploded in flames on the freeway, and their children inside were engulfed and consumed in an instant. As they sat before those microphones, and the world listened in for insight as to whether their faith could remain in such tragedy, they began by quoting **Psalm 34:1: "I will bless the Lord at all times; His praise shall continually be in my mouth."** The Word of God was their anchor in a storm that would have quickly capsized most of the boats. From the most successful athletes to people of quiet faith in the hidden corners of the globe, God's Word is a constant and reliable source of stability in the toughest of times. Are you experiencing that stability?

And One More Thing

God's Word promises justice. Deep within the heart of every person on the face of the earth is a sense of right and wrong and a longing for justice—both personally and in our world. God made us to look for and long for true justice. **Psalm 19:9b (NKJV) says, "The judgments of**

the LORD are true and righteous altogether." Sometimes we suppress that God-given hunger for justice, but just when we think we have it put down, we will read of a rape or hear of a murder, and something hidden inside our very being rises up within us and yearns for wrong to be punished. And as we see crime and evil in our society escalating at a sickening pace, our yearning for justice becomes terrifically difficult to cope with.

There used to be a little feature in *Reader's Digest* called "That's Outrageous." Here were true stories, specific accounts of people who had been severely wronged, telling how our society and our government failed to administer the justice due. Criminals out of jail early, committing the horrendous. Murderers let off on a technicality and freed to murder again, all under the banner of justice. Anyway I had to quit reading the feature; it was just too upsetting. How do you cope with this? The only way I know is to keep in mind that we have a God of perfect justice. **"The judgments of the LORD are true and righteous altogether."** The word *judgments* describes God's verdicts, pronouncements of consequence, and punishment for sin. When God makes a judgment, it is true and altogether righteous. Though the final judgment of God is yet future, the Bible tells us what His verdicts will be. God is not capricious like our human judges; He doesn't operate according to His moods or personal circumstances. We can be sure that He will judge fairly and precisely, consistent with all He has told us in Scripture. Those are His judgments, and we cannot expect a continuance.

Have you got the six statements? Look at the chart below and take a moment to review all that God Himself promises His Word to be.

The law of the Lord is so comprehensive that it's able to totally transform the inner person.

God's testimony about Himself is so reliable that it can take a vacillating simpleton and make him or her skilled in daily living.

God's divine principles set a right path through the maze of life and cause our hearts to rejoice.

The commands of God are so crystal-clear that they bring light to the darkness in every human heart.

The fear of the Lord is without blemish and brings stability to every person in every generation who turns to Him.

The judgments of the Lord set a path of justice through human history that will ultimately right every wrong and silence every rebel.

BETTER THAN MONEY AND HONEY

Psalm 19:10 concludes by saying, **"More to be desired are they than gold, yea, than much fine gold; sweeter also than honey and the honeycomb."** That is quite a statement when you think of it. God is promising that His Word, when properly understood for what it is and truly experienced on a heart level, is worth more than gold. In fact, it's worth more than "much fine gold." Beyond that, God's Word will become very sweet to you, sweeter than honey. Together these two pictures of honey and money mean that God's Word will satisfy you more than the earthly things you might be tempted to put in its place.

Finally, we are told that through Scripture **". . . Your servant is warned, and in keeping them there is great reward" (v. 11).** We need to be warned. Life is a like a minefield, and God's Word is the map to safety. When you obey God's commands, you discover "in keeping them there is great reward." Of course God makes sure that everyone who neglects His Word ultimately regrets it, and everyone who learns it and lives it and loves it is greatly rewarded.

I could write for years about the benefits of the Bible, but the bottom line is this: God wrote a book! That book is totally sufficient for all that we need in life. And if you have read this far, then you must be asking how you can get these incredible benefits out of the Bible for yourself and your family. That is the subject of the next chapter, and I can't wait to go there *with* you!

4

How to Benefit from the Bible

*Your words were found and I ate them, and
Your words became for me a joy and the delight
of my heart; for I have been called by Your
name, O Lord God of hosts.*

JEREMIAH 15:16

W hen growing up, I always used to watch game shows. They were on early in the morning, and during the lazy, hazy days of summer when I was having a hard time getting my little motor going, I would vegetate for an hour or two and watch my favorite shows—$10,000 Pyramid, Match Game, The Price Is Right, and another one I sort of remember with life-size playing cards. Probably my most favorite though was the show where the winner gets to go on a one-minute shopping spree in a grocery store and fill as many carts as possible in the allotted time. Kids love food, and my friends and I used to debate about what we could grab in sixty seconds. I used to love watching the people all fired up, getting all they could "while the getting was good."

Having read the first three chapters, you now understand the incredible treasure that we have in God's Word. You also understand what a monumental resource it is to fill your life with joy and fulfillment in the maximum way our Creator intended. If you really understand what the Bible is and does for us, then you should be like a dying woman who has just found the cure. You should be like a starving man at the Country Buffet. You should be just as fired up as one of those crazy game-show contestants with the grocery cart in front of them, waiting for the bell to sound. You should be ready to *lay hold* of the Word of God.

You say, "Well, if the Bible is so great, then why aren't more people reading it?" That's a very good question. Often when I am studying and preparing a message for the people in my church, I will do an informal questionnaire to find out why people do what they do. Here's one of them—we surveyed a bunch of people with this question: "Name a reason you've heard for not reading the Bible." Here are the top three answers:

• *Number three*: "It's old and boring." I know some people feel this way, but that's because they don't know how to study Scripture for themselves (or they have been listening to an apathetic preacher). I have never met a person who knows how to study the Bible and is doing it who would say the Bible is a sleeper—quite the opposite, in fact.

• *Number two*: "I forget to read it." These people leave church fired up about the Bible, but by the time Monday rolls around, they are occupied with other things. The Bible gets lost in the shuffle. Like most of us, they are acknowledging that good things often crowd the best and most profitable things out of their schedule.

• *Number one*: "I don't understand it." People say this because they pick the wrong place to start. They think, *Well, I've heard of the book of Revelation; so maybe I'll start there.* Let me tell you, picking up the Bible and starting in Revelation is like asking a first grader to begin with algebra or calculus! Until you've done $2 + 2 = 4$, you can't do calculus. And until you've read the Gospel of John and some other basic passages, you cannot do the book of Revelation. With a good strategy of where to begin, you *will* understand the Bible.

In this chapter I want to address those reasons. I want to help you get beyond knowing about the Bible, maybe even believing that it can help you. I believe you can get to the point where you actually know how to benefit from the Bible yourself. So no more background, no more context — you have learned enough now to begin to experience the Bible on your own. Everything you have read so far has been to get you to this critical stage of moving from knowledge to action. Do these three things with God's Word, and your life will be changed.

#1 PICK IT UP!

If you want to benefit from the Bible, you've got to pick it up. It's not doing any good on your desk. It's not helping anyone on your shelf. It doesn't matter if you have a nice Bible on the coffee table or a great one in the glove compartment of your car. The Bible is not some magical book that will do its work hanging in a little box around your neck or in a shirt pocket close to your heart. In order to benefit from the Bible, you've got to *pick it up!*

Nothing is sadder to me than the number of Bibles sitting unread in countless homes because the inhabitants have never truly understood or recognized that God did indeed write that book. Take a moment and read The

Diary of a Bible, and see if you recognize some patterns in your life that need to change.

THE DIARY OF A BIBLE

- January 15. Been resting for a week. A few nights after the first of the year, my owner opened me, but no more. Another New Year's resolution gone wrong.
- February 3. Owner picked me up and rushed off to Sunday school.
- February 23. Cleaning day. Dusted and put back in my place.
- April 2. Busy day. Owner had to present the lesson at a church society meeting. Quickly looked up a lot of references.
- May 5. Grandma's in town. Back in her lap. A very comfortable place.
- May 9. She let a tear fall on John 14.
- May 10. Grandma's gone. Back in my old place again.
- May 20. Baby born. They wrote his name on one of my pages.
- July 1. Packed in a suitcase. Off for a vacation.
- July 20. Still in the suitcase. Almost everything else taken out.

- July 25. Home again. Quite a journey, though I don't see why I went.
- August 16. Dusted again and put in a prominent place. The minister is to be here for dinner.
- August 20. Owner wrote Grandma's death in the Family Record. He left his extra pair of glasses between my pages.
- December 31. Owner just found his glasses. Wonder if he will make any resolutions about me for the new year?[1]

What story would your Bible tell? Are you reading your Bible daily? Are you memorizing portions, hiding them in your heart? Are you obeying the Bible? Are you letting it guide your life? **Psalm 119:105 says, "Your word is a lamp to my feet and a light to my path."**

I was talking to a leader in my church, and he told me about a recent business trip. He had been working pretty hard; so when he got on the plane, he found a quiet seat in a corner at the back and settled in to spend some time feeding his soul from God's Word. Later as he walked off the plane, he told of feeling refreshed and encouraged by his time in the Word. He said, "I couldn't help but notice that littering the seats were all kinds of papers and magazines: *USA Today, Wall Street Journal, Chicago Tribune, New York Times.*

They had been read and thrown down, and that was the end of it. But under my arm—and in my heart—was the eternal Word of God. **"The grass withers, the flower fades, but the word of our God stands forever" (Isaiah 40:8).**

Let me ask you: How many times this week have you touched a newspaper? How many times have you held a magazine? How many times did you aim the remote control (I can never find the stinking thing!)? How often did you touch the keys of your computer? But in comparison, how many times did you pick up the book that God wrote? We make all kinds of time for the words of men, and yet we're too busy to read the Word of God. Everything good starts with this: You have to pick it up! You may have wondered as I often do: *Hey, if the Bible is so great, why aren't more people picking it up?* In fact, I am so excited about where this chapter is headed that I want to suggest that you get a Bible right now before we go any further. Do you own one? If not, buy one from a local bookstore, or for versions in languages other than English, contact the website www.gospelcom.net/ibs/. The Bible comes in many sizes, shapes, and versions. You can explore those for yourself at some point, but to make it easy for you, get a Bible with no study notes or extensive references. I would suggest you buy the English Standard Version: englishstandardversion.org or 1-800-635-7993. It is an essentially literal translation and yet quite readable.[2] I hope you have a Bible actually in your hands. If so, you have taken the first step toward changing your life for the better. None of the wonderful benefits will ever be yours without that all-important first step. You've got to *pick it up!*

#2 SIZE IT UP.

This statement is about valuing the Bible for what it is. I remember the first time I bought a car. I didn't have much money, and I was only a few weeks away from my wedding day; so I wanted to be sure I made the right decision. The car I had chosen was a 1983 Ford Escort. I had the down payment and could handle the monthly amount, but still I wasn't sure. Again and again I walked around the car — checking the tires, scanning for scratches, examining the grill and the taillights. Before I jumped in with both feet, I had to size it up.

To some degree that's what this whole book has been about. But in another very real sense, you size up the Bible every time you pick it up. It's as if before you crack the cover, you sort of hold it up on the tips of your fingers and walk around it. To help you size up your Bible, I want to share eight biblical pictures of God's Word. If you rightly understand the pictures — the things God

Himself says about His Word — you can't help but value this book. Here's the first one:

FIRE

The Bible is fire, and many places in Scripture we are told as much. **"Therefore, thus says the LORD, the God of Hosts, 'Because you have spoken this word, behold, I am making My words in your mouth fire and this people wood, and it will consume them'"** (Jeremiah 5:14). WOW!

I experience the reality of that Scripture on a weekly basis. I get the privilege of standing before thousands of people with God's Word in my mouth and seeing the incredible impact that it makes. I see the truth penetrate their hearts, grip their minds, move their emotions, and, best of all, engage their wills toward transformation. God's Word *is* like fire; it *consumes* people's hearts. The text says that you will be like wood, kindling thrown upon a blaze. If you'll give it even half a chance, it will *burn* the *dross* and the useless things out of your life so fast. God's Word is fire!

SWORD

This is a picture I have held in my mind since childhood. In Sunday school we used to have these things called Sword Drills. The teacher was helping us learn to use our

Bibles and look up specific verses. We would hold our
Bibles over our heads (we called them swords), and we
would all say the reference together. The teacher would
yell, "Charge," and the first kid to look it up and stand
was allowed to read the passage aloud and would get
points toward a prize. It was so much fun. That picture
of our Bibles as swords has never left me.

The idea is based upon **Hebrews 4:12a (ESV): "For
the word of God is living and active, sharper than any
two-edged sword."** Not a knife or dagger, not a spear,
but a sword. The weapon of hand-to-hand combat. In
fact, **Ephesians 6:17 says, "And take . . . the sword of the
spirit, which is the word of God."** When Satan is trying
to tempt us or discourage us, it's the Word of God we
use to defeat him. Amazingly, Jesus Christ Himself, the
second person of the Trinity, used the Word of God as a
sword to deflect the temptations of the enemy (Matthew
4:1-11). Can we afford to do less? You say, "Sometimes
the fire doesn't get my attention." Well, the sword will,
because the Bible describes this sword as **"piercing to
the division of soul and of spirit, of joints and of marrow, and discerning the thoughts and intentions of the
heart" (Hebrews 4:12b ESV).** The sword of God's Word
quickly cuts to the heart of the matter.

I can't tell you how many times people come up after

I have preached God's Word and ask, "Dude, did someone call you? Did someone tell you what's going on in my
life? I am *so* mad at my wife right now! She called you,
didn't she? She wrote you a letter and told you what's
been going on!" Then I have to explain that it's not that I
know their secrets; it's the Word of God discerning their
thoughts. Why should we be surprised? This is God's
book, and as His Spirit takes His Word, it's like a sword.
It pierces us, it penetrates us, it prescribes the specific
answers right when and right where we need them.

HAMMER

**Jeremiah 23:29 (ESV) says, "Is not my word like . . . a
hammer that breaks the rock in pieces?"** The Word of
God is a hammer. Possibly as you are reading this, you
have been thinking to yourself, *The Bible has never been
a fire or a sword to me.* If that is true, it is because your
heart has become very hard, and so the Word of God
bounces off your heart like BBs hitting a concrete wall.
You need to be very careful about a hard heart because
if God can't get to you with the fire or the sword, guess
what? The hammer's going to fall. God says, **"My word
. . . [is] like a hammer that breaks the rock in pieces."**
Many of those whose lives have been changed by the
Word of God reference a time when their hearts were

very hard, and God had to break them, and it was very painful. Nobody wants to meet the hammer of God's Word bringing conviction and change. That is why the Scripture exhorts us, **"Today, if you would hear His voice, do not harden your hearts" (Psalm 95:7-8)**.

SEED

Here's a picture of incredible value: God's Word is seed. **"Having been born again, not of corruptible seed but incorruptible, through the word of God which lives and abides forever" (1 Peter 1:23 NKJV)**. In one of His parables Jesus said, **"The seed is the word of God" (Luke 8:11 NKJV)**.

One of the many things I adore about my wife is her love for gardening. She is so patient and forward-thinking when in the spring she goes out into the garden and plants her seed in the ground. Nothing much happens at first, but over time those little seeds burst forth in one or another beautiful life form, plants and flowers, and we enjoy them for the whole summer as we sit out back.

The picture of the Bible as seed has many applications. Which ones come to your mind? I think of how a seed starts so small and takes time to grow, needing continual attention. Similarly the Word of God starts to work in our hearts, but it takes time. Sometimes we have to hear the same thing several times before it really starts to connect. In the same way God's Word planted in the human heart will bear much fruit and bring much beauty over time, but it requires a willingness to plant the seed by faith and wait.

MILK

The Word of God is milk. When I think of milk, I think of something refreshing and nourishing. I remember how our three precious children, each getting so big now, used to crave and cry for their milk. You didn't have to give them any instruction about the fact that they needed milk; they were born with their mouths open. What mother's milk was to our little babies, so the Word of God is in the life of a sincere person of faith. In **1 Peter 2:2**, we learn, **"like newborn babies, long for the pure milk of the word, so that by it you may grow."** I don't see people crying very often because they haven't been fed physically, but how many are filled with anxiety and fear and discouragement because they have neglected God's only provision for their spiritual nourishment.

MEAT

Do you remember when you stopped drinking milk? As a kid I couldn't get enough of it, maybe two or three glasses every day. Then when I became a teen, I cut way down to maybe two or three glasses a week. Today I am almost forty-two, and I bet I don't drink more than one or two glasses of milk per month. In the same way there are portions of God's Word that are milk. We never outgrow them, but they are the foundation for meatier truth that is the substance we need to keep growing in our faith. Milk is like the elementary or basic things of the Bible: The Bible is God's Word; Jesus is our Savior; we can have our sins forgiven; we are supposed to love other people; we are supposed to forgive other people. That's milk.

Hebrews 5:12-14 says, **"For though by this time you ought to be teachers, you have need again for someone to teach you the elementary principles of the oracles of God, and you have come to need milk and not solid food. For everyone who partakes only of milk is not accustomed to the word of righteousness."** Are you hearing that? *Everyone who partakes only of milk is unskilled in the Word of God.* The passage goes on to say, **"But solid food is for the mature, who because of practice, have their senses trained to discern good and evil."** If you've known Christ for any amount of time at all, you begin to find yourself saying, "Isn't there more? Isn't there more?" The answer is yes! There is more—the meat of

God's Word. We cannot exist only on milk; we have to have meat, and God's Word can be meat to us.

LIGHT

In **Psalm 119:105** we read: **"Your Word is a lamp to my feet and a light to my path."** Now here's the great thing about light. If you're walking around in the dark, you stumble over stuff and hurt yourself. The Word of God works in our lives in such a way that we don't walk down dark alleys anymore and find ourselves at dead ends, getting ripped off. We don't make dumb mistakes and think, *Well, this would be a great thing to do with my life.* No! The light of God's Word shines on our path and says, "Don't go there. Bad plan." If you know what it is to be perplexed about an important decision hanging over your head, then you understand the value of having God's Word to light your path.

MIRROR

God's Word is also a mirror. Sometimes the problem isn't something out there that I might trip over. Sometimes the problem is in my own heart. That's why I'm thankful that the Word of God is also a mirror. **James 1:23-25** says, **"For if anyone is a hearer of the word and not a doer, he is like a man who looks at his natural face in a mir-**

ror; for once he has looked at himself and gone away, he has immediately forgotten what kind of person he was. But one who looks intently at the perfect law, the law of liberty, and abides by it, not having become a forgetful hearer but an effectual doer, this man will be blessed in what he does."

Notice the phrase: "For if anyone is a hearer of the word and not a doer, he is like a man who looks at his natural face in a mirror." God's Word shows us ourselves! It confronts us with truth and convicts us about our true need. Now what's the most foolish thing you can do when you look in a mirror? If, for example, I have a blob of mustard on my face and, after looking in the mirror, forget to rub it off, how silly would that make me? So the real power then is not in the words exclusively but in my doing what the Word of God says.

There are eight things, then, that the Bible tells us to help us size it up. We have taken a moment to hold the Bible up on our fingers and walk around it one last time. Maybe we have a readiness like we have never known before to pick up the Bible and to study it for ourselves. So now I want to cover that third and all-important step. First we pick it up, then we size it up, and finally we:

#3 EAT IT UP!

I'm sure that's a new concept to you, and I promise it's not some mystical, weird thing. **Jeremiah 15:16** says, **"Your words were found and I ate them, and Your words became for me a joy and the delight of my heart."** Several of the "value pictures" we just discussed speak of the Word of God as consumable, i.e., milk, meat, seed (sort of), and the Word of God is also described as bread. So the idea of eating it is not really that strange. What food is to our bodies, Scripture is to our souls. So here are five things you need to do if you want to eat God's Word and feed your soul.

READ IT

If you pick it up and size it up but don't read it, well, what a waste, right? So open it and begin to read. You say, "Dude, it has hundreds of pages. Where should I start?" I hear that so often that I decided to check the Bibles I own. They average around 1,400 pages. So think of the Bible as two big books or four to five regular-sized books. Studies indicate that the Bible takes about seventy hours to read out loud. Most people read a little faster than that, but the Bible is not a book you want to read quickly anyway. It's sort of like your favorite dessert—take a bite or two and put the spoon down—a good way to make sure you are comprehending the power of what you are reading. If you read it for twelve minutes per day, or one and a half hours per week, you would have no problem finishing the Bible in a year, and you would be so incredibly blessed you would want to start all over again the next year. Reading the Bible is really not as intimidating as most people make it.

As for *where* to start, I have always recommended that people begin in the Gospel of John, which is the fourth book in the New Testament, the fourth eyewitness account of the life of Jesus. As you read slowly through this Gospel, stop to underline the word *believe* every time you see it and ask yourself: Believe what? Or believe whom? Then go to 1, 2, and 3 John. Then look at another Gospel. That'll keep you busy for a while. Have a brief word of prayer before you begin to read. Ask the Lord to open your mind and heart to His truth and then believe that He will. Also, don't lie down when you read the Bible. It's not a magazine or a dime store novel. Remember, it's God's Word, and if you give it the respect it deserves, it will "rock your world" in an incredible way. If you use a serious posture, you'll get a serious result. Read it. I suggest taking at least fifteen minutes to go through two or three chapters at a time.

Here's a second thing. Don't *just* read it:

QUESTION IT

Because you're just starting out, I'll suggest some questions, and over time you can develop your own.

1. **"What portion of my reading stands out to me?"** You'll read two or three chapters, and you'll feel drawn back to a certain part. Go back to that part and ask the following questions.

2. **"Why does this part have my attention?"** What is it about this that has caught my attention? To help you answer that question, use the remaining questions.

3. **"Is there an example for me to follow?"** I can't tell you how many times God's Word has impacted my life just from my saying these simple words: "Is there an example for me to follow?" All of a sudden it's like—BOOM!—it jumps right off the page. "James, you should be more like that!" And I love it when God's Word speaks to me in this way and calls me to be more of what the Lord requires.

4. **"Is there an error for me to avoid?"** It's very comforting to know that if I have unknowingly stepped in a wrong direction or made an unwise decision, God's Word can reveal that to me. It's easy to see the mistakes others make, but much harder to see our own mistakes. This is where the Word of God becomes that "mirror" we talked about earlier. Is there an error for me to avoid?

5. **"Is there a duty for me to perform?"** Is there an action that God's Word is calling me to take? Is there

some matter of importance that I am neglecting in my home or where I work or in regard to my personal life? If so, I want to know what it is so I can work on it. God's Word will often reveal to us a duty to perform.

6. **"Is there any promise for me to claim?"** So often God's Word brings strength and encouragement. As you study the Bible, you will hear the Lord committing Himself to certain things or to act in certain ways. As you come to those promises, you might just acknowledge, "Yes, God! You are like this, and You've promised to be this way for all my life, and I trust You." Your heart will be thrilled as you learn and review the promises of God.

7. **"Is there a sin for me to confess?"** This I suppose is obvious in some respects. You won't read the Bible long until you come across many passages that reveal to you the "error of your ways." But one of the promises that helps with that is **1 John 1:9** esv, which says, **"If we confess our sins, he is faithful and just to forgive us our sins and to cleanse us from all unrighteousness."**

Now as you begin to question God's Word, you're going to be ready to do this third thing.

Plan It

This is absolutely essential if you are going to benefit from the Bible as much as you could for the rest of your life. Make a plan of action regarding how you will implement what you are learning. Have a journal open beside your Bible and write some notes. Write some thoughts in the margin of your Bible. When the word convicts you about anger or deceit or selfishness, have a strategy to deal with those sins. Make your plan specific and measurable. The results you begin to see will amaze you. Read it. Question it. Plan it.

PRAY IT

So often people are unsure of what to say in personal prayer. When you are praying back the truths of God's own Word, you can be confident you are praying as God would have you do. You can also be confident that God will respond to what you are asking if the direction truly comes from His Word. That's what it means to pray according to God's will. How I wish I had read a book this specific and practical twenty years ago. It would have helped me so much. Instead I banged around for a long time before I figured this stuff out. Anyway, at least you can learn from my mistakes. There is an incredible power when you pray God's Word back to Him. When you open the passage and say, "God, You're this way, and You've promised to always be this way." Wow! So read it. Question it. Plan it. Pray it.

SHARE IT

When you've learned something from God's Word, you *have* to share it with somebody else. Take time to relay something about your study to your spouse or your roommate or to a friend at school. Maybe you could share with a co-worker or someone at your church. **Hebrews 10:24** says that we are supposed to **"consider how to stimulate one another to love and good deeds."** That is what happens when you share what you are getting out of God's Word. People who hear me preach and see my enthusiasm think, *Man, that guy really loves to preach.* But I don't. I hardly care about preaching at all — at least not as an end in itself. What fires me up is hearing about the difference that God's Word makes in people's lives. If I got up each Sunday and preached, knowing that nobody would apply it, I wouldn't even show. That's the truth. The reason we share God's Word is not for ourselves; it's for others. Then, as a by-product, we get the incredible blessing of seeing almighty God use it.

The Scripture says in **Isaiah 40:8, "The grass withers, the flower fades, but the word of our God stands forever."** Someday when your television and your car and your whole house are on the garbage heap, the truth in this one book will still be alive. Now let's invest ourselves in the one thing that lasts. I want to say it again: God wrote a book. May God forgive us for not making better use of it in our lives.

WHY ONE MORE CHAPTER?

Maybe you're like, "Okay, I've got it! I don't need you to keep going on and on about this." I agree—it really is simple. That's why I have tried to keep this book short. We have seen the evidence for the Bible as God's Word. We have covered the history of how the Bible actually came into being and how the individual books were compiled into one big book. We spent a whole chapter learning about the things God promises His Word will do in your life, and now we've spent a chapter on how you can extract those benefits from the Bible for yourself. I know it seems like we should be done, and you *are* almost ready to dig in to the Bible, but without the last chapter, you could be spinning your wheels for a long time. Really! So just a few more pages, and you're off to the races.

5

Jesus, the Message of the Bible

Forever, O Lord, Your word is settled in heaven.

PSALM 119:89 NASB

I suppose that I could have put this at the end of the last chapter but what I am about to say is so important that I wanted to make sure it would not get lost in the midst of all we have been learning about the Bible.

It's Not a Destination

In light of everything that has been said so far in this book, it might surprise you to learn that the Bible is not an end in itself. The Bible is not a destination; it's a bridge to a better place. That place is a personal relationship with Jesus Christ. We don't worship a book; we worship the One who wrote the book. The first four chapters of my book cover what theologians call Bibliology. But if we are not careful, Bibliology can easily cross over into bibliolatry. That's where, rather than studying the Bible, we worship it.

EVER HEARD OF THE PHARISEES?

The Pharisees were a first-century religious sect that prided themselves on their adherence to the literal Word of God. The Pharisees were the most religious people of their day, the most involved, the most devout. They memorized lengthy portions of the Old Testament and gave their lives to learning "every jot and tittle," which were parts of Hebrew punctuation. They were so fond of Scripture that they actually wore it as a fashion statement in bracelets and headbands called phylacteries (Matthew 23:5). If we didn't know better, we might have thought that these would be the ones most likely to welcome God's Son when He came to the earth as the long-promised Messiah. Instead they argued with Jesus, resisted Him, falsely accused Him, and ultimately carried out their plot of murder by crucifixion. Yes, that's what these "lovers of God's Word" did.

How Can That Be?

You may wonder how religious leaders so committed to God's Word could commit such blind wickedness. The secret to their blindness is revealed in a conversation Christ had with them. Two separate times we read in John 5 that they were persecuting Jesus and trying to kill Him (vv. 16, 18). In response Jesus said, **"You search the Scriptures because you think that in them you have eternal life; it is these that testify about Me" (John 5:39).** In fact, just before that He had told them explicitly that God's Word could not abide in them because they did not believe in Him, the One God had sent (v. 38).

Here's the Point

Jesus is the message of the Bible. As a kid I used to sing a little chorus my mother taught me:

> *The Bible is the written Word of God.*
> *It tells about the living Word of God.*
> *On every page, on every line,*
> *you'll find the Son of God divine.*
> *If you want to learn to know*
> *   the King of kings,*
> *if you want to learn of all*
> *   the heavenly things —*
> *read the book, learn the book,*
> *   let the book teach you!*

The point is that if you are not growing in your knowledge of Christ, then you are failing to achieve God's purpose for giving you the Bible, no matter what else you may be learning from it. The purpose of the Bible is that we might be reconciled to God through faith in His Son: **"For God so loved the world, that He gave His only begotten Son, that whoever believes in Him shall not perish, but have eternal life" (John 3:16).**

Now I know some will try to say that they can study the Bible and remain uninterested in a personal relationship with Jesus, but that is simply not so. The Bible teaches that all of us are sinful: **"For all have sinned and fall short of the glory of God" (Romans 3:23).** Because of the sinful condition we were born into and now exist in, we are completely and utterly unable to understand God's Word. Oh, you may be able to comprehend the meaning of the words, but its deep spiritual impact, all that I described in chapters 3 and 4, will never be experienced in your life unless you invite God to forgive you for your sin and so remove that barrier to your understanding. **First Corinthians 2:14** says that the **"natural man** [a person still in the sinful condition we are all born with] **does not accept the things of the Spirit of God, for they are foolishness to him; and he cannot understand them."**

COULD THAT BE YOUR STRUGGLE?

Possibly you relate very much to that verse in 1 Corinthians. Maybe you have had a growing interest in the message of the Bible, but for some reason it has never really "clicked" for you. Maybe you would even be so honest as to say that you have often thought the message of the Bible to be just so much foolishness. That's because you are still a "natural man" or "natural woman"; you are still in the sinful spiritual condition in which you were born.

HOW DO I CHANGE THAT?

The book of Romans goes on to say that the wages for our sin, or what we get for what we have done, is death (Romans 6:23). For those who remain in the "natural" state, there is a hopeless future and an eternity separated from God in an awful place called hell. "But how could a God of love send anyone to a place called hell?" you might ask. Hell is not actually a statement about God's love; it is a statement about God's holiness. **Exodus 34:7** says that while God is one **"who keeps lovingkindness for thousands, who forgives iniquity, transgression and sin; yet He will by no means leave *the guilty* unpunished."** Just because God is loving does not mean He will casually disregard our sins. While hell is a statement about God's holiness, Christ and the cross are a statement about God's love.

Take a moment and read these Scriptures:

Romans 5:8 – But God demonstrates His own love toward us, in that while we were yet sinners, Christ died for us.

1 John 4:10 – In this is love, not that we loved God, but that He loved us and sent His Son to be the propitiation for our sins.

2 Corinthians 5:21 – He made Him who knew no sin to be sin on our behalf, so that we might become the righteousness of God in Him.

John 5:24 – Truly, truly, I say to you, he who hears My word, and believes Him who sent Me, has eternal life, and does not come into judgment, but has passed out of death into life.

John 1:12 – But as many as received Him, to them He gave the right to become children of God, even to those who believe in His name.

Some Closing Questions

If you have read this far, then you must sense that I care for you and have prayed much for you even as I have been writing this book. I also know that you must be very interested in understanding the Bible—and you can. God will help you if you commit or recommit to a personal relationship with His Son. To help you do that, let me ask you a few questions. I encourage you to answer them as sincerely as you can.

Do you believe that Jesus is God's Son?

Do you believe that He died on the cross to pay the penalty for your sins?

Do you believe that if you turn from your sin and by faith ask God to forgive you, that God will, in fact, do that?

Would you be willing to pray a prayer of confession and commitment right now along those lines?

A Prayer for Coming to Christ

"I know that I am a sinner and deserve Your rejection and punishment. Thank You for loving me enough to send Your Son Jesus into this world to die as payment for my sin. I repent of my sin and turn to You alone for my forgiveness. I believe that You are the only One who can cleanse my heart and change me. I now receive Jesus as the Savior and Lord of my life. Today I am making the choice to convert to following You and Your truth. Thank You for forgiving my sins and opening my mind to understand Your Word. In the name of Jesus I pray. Amen."

What Now?

Now you are ready to dig into God's Word for yourself.

You understand why the Bible is a unique book, unlike any other.

You understand where the Bible came from and how it was written.

You understand what the benefits of the Bible are and the difference it can make in your life.

You understand its value and how to access that for yourself: Pick it up, size it up, and eat it up.

Best of all, you have a confirmed relationship with the Author!

You can understand it because the power of Christ is now at work within you. You can study the Bible as far more than just a cool book. You can understand, believe, and obey it as THE BOOK GOD WROTE.

APPENDIX

To get the most from your Bible reading, here are some questions to use in your study. They will help you draw the meaning from a passage and apply it to your life. You might wish to tear this page out and put it in your Bible.

1. "What portion of my reading stands out to me?"
2. "Why does this part have my attention?"
3. "Is there an example for me to follow?"
4. "Is there an error for me to avoid?"
5. "Is there a duty for me to perform?"
6. "Is there any promise for me to claim?"
7. "Is there a sin for me to confess?"

NOTES

Evidence for the Bible You Shouldn't Ignore

1. Source: United Bible Society, *Scripture Language Report 2000*, posted at *www.Biblesociety.org/wr_358/slr_2000.htm*, as accessed on 1/29/02.
2. Source: *www.biblesociety.org.uk*, as accessed on 1/29/02.
3. Source: *www.gideons.org*, as accessed on 1/29/02.
4. Bernard Ramm, *Protestant Christian Evidences* (Chicago: Moody Press, 1957), 239, cited in Josh McDowell, *The Best of Josh McDowell: A Ready Defense*, comp. Bill Wilson (Nashville: Thomas Nelson, 1993), 32-33.
5. Cited at *www.why-the-Bible.com/Bible.htm*, as accessed on 1/29/02. I must admit that Professor Williams's opinion, though learned, is nevertheless an opinion. Those who do not share my presuppositions will not find it as convincing as the other proofs.
6. Norman Geisler and William E. Nix, *A General Introduction to the Bible* (Chicago: Moody Press, 1968), 123-24.
7. Josh McDowell, *The New Evidence That Demands a Verdict* (Nashville: Nelson, 1999), 34.
8. David S. Dockery, Kenneth A. Mathews, and Robert B. Sloan, *Foundations for Biblical Interpretation* (Nashville: Broadman & Holman, 1994), 182, cited in Josh McDowell, *New Evidence*, 35.
9. Cited in McDowell, *Best of Josh McDowell*, 23.
10. McDowell, *New Evidence*, 38.
11. Most evangelical scholars hold that only the writings of John were completed at that late date; there are good reasons to believe that the remaining New Testament books were completed prior to A.D. 70. See D. A. Carson, Douglas J. Moo, and Leon Morris, *An Introduction to the New Testament* (Grand Rapids: Zondervan, 1992).
12. McDowell, *New Evidence*, 38.
13. Geisler and Nix, *General Introduction*, 263.

14. *Christianity Today,* September 7, 1998. The quote is taken from the front cover.
15. William F. Albright, *The Archaeology of Palestine,* rev. ed. (Harmondsworth, Middlesex: Pelican Books, 1960), 127-28; cited in McDowell, *Best of Josh McDowell,* 92.
16. For a detailed account by one of the site's chief archaeologists, see Giovanni Pettinato, *Ebla: A New Look at History* (Baltimore: Johns Hopkins University Press, 1991).
17. For a general overview of Hittite culture, see O. R. Gurney, *The Hittites,* rev. ed. (Baltimore: Penguin, 1991).
18. For other examples of this, see Victor H. Matthews and Don C. Benjamin, *Old Testament Parallels: Laws and Stories from the Ancient Near East* (New York: Paulist Press, 1991), 46-51.
19. For a good example of how the scholarly consensus can change as a result of archaeological work, see Bryant G. Wood, "Did the Israelites Conquer Jericho? A New Look at the Archaeological Evidence," *Biblical Archaeology Review* 16 (March/April 1990): 44-59.
20. Hershel Shanks, "'David' Found at Dan," *Biblical Archaeology Review* 20 (March/April 1994): 26-39; Andre Lemaire, "'House of David' Restored in Moabite Inscription," *Biblical Archaeology Review* 20 (May/June 1994): 30ff.; David Noel Freedman and Jeffrey C. Geoghegan, "'House of David' Is There!" *Biblical Archaeology Review* 21 (March/April 1995): 78-79.
21. James K. Hoffmeier, *Israel in Egypt: The Evidence for the Authenticity of the Exodus Tradition* (New York: Oxford University Press, 1996).
22. For a sampling of the evidence for a six-day creation, see John F. Ashton, ed., *In Six Days: Why Fifty Scientists Choose to Believe in Creation* (Green Forest, Ark.: New Leaf Press, 2000), and James B. Jordan, *Creation in Six Days: A Defense of the Traditional Reading of Genesis One* (Moscow, Idaho: Canon Press, 1999).
23. I have mentioned only four here. The others are enumerated in McDowell, *New Evidence,* 168-92.
24. Peter W. Stoner and Robert C. Newman, *Science Speaks* (Chicago: Moody, 1976), 106-12; cited in McDowell, *Best of Josh McDowell,* 213.

Where Did the Bible Come From?

1. These figures are actually based on the King James Version of the Bible, not the original Greek and Hebrew manuscripts.
2. Charles C. Ryrie, *A Survey of Bible Doctrine* (Chicago: Moody Press, 1972), 40.

3.   I am not against using secondary sources, like commentaries, introductions, surveys, and systematic theologies. These tools can help us understand God's Word better, particularly when we are unsure about the meaning of a particular verse. I simply do not believe that they should be included on the same page as the biblical text, lest they receive the same amount of respect and credulity.

4.   I wrote this with the help of my friend Chris Seay.

5.   This does not mean that these men were perfect. On the contrary, they were sinners just as we are. Yet despite their faults and shortcomings, these men had hearts for God. They grieved when they sinned, and they sought God's forgiveness. And God bestowed on them the privilege of writing His Word.

6.   Norman Geisler and William E. Nix, *A General Introduction to the Bible* (Chicago: Moody Press, 1968).

What Is the Bible Good For?

1.   For instance, writing for the American Psychological Association about the so-called scientific nature of psychology, Sigmund Koch concluded, "The *hope* of a psychological science became indistinguishable from the *fact* of psychological science. The entire subsequent history of psychology can be seen as a ritualistic endeavor to emulate the forms of science in order to sustain the delusion that it already is a science." Sigmund Koch and David E. Leary, eds., *A Century of Psychology as Science* (American Psychological Association, 1992).

2.   In my treatment of this passage, I am indebted to a message that I heard many years ago by Dr. John MacArthur.

3.   Charles Haddon Spurgeon, *Treasury of David* (Grand Rapids: Zondervan, 1940), 87.

How to Benefit from the Bible

1.   Author unknown.

2.   It is worth noting that I gain nothing by promoting the ESV; I recommend it because we use it at our church.

INDEX